W9-CCI-108

After Theory

Also by Terry Eagleton

After Theory

TERRY EAGLETON

BASIC
BOOKS

A Member of the Perseus Books Group
New York

In memory of my mother

Rosaleen Riley

(1913–2002)

Copyright © 2003 by Terry Eagleton

Published by Basic Books
A Member of the Perseus Books Group

All rights reserved. Printed in the United States of America. First published in the United Kingdom by Allen Lane, an imprint of Penguin Books Ltd, London, in 2003. No part of this book may be reproduced in any manner whatsoever without written permission except in the case of brief quotations embodied in critical articles and reviews. For information, contact Basic Books, 387 Park Aveune South, New York, NY 10016-8810.

Books published by Basic Books are available at special discounts for bulk purchases in the United States by corporations, institutions, and other organizations. For more information, please contact the Special Markets Department at the Perseus Books Group, 11 Cambridge Center, Cambridge MA 02142, or call (617) 252-5298, (800) 255-1514, or e-mail j.mccrary@perseusbooks.com

Typeset in 11.25/15.25 pt PostScript Linotype Sabon

A CIP catalog record for this book is available from the Library of Congress

ISBN 0–465–01773–8

04 05 / 10 9 8 7 6 5 4 3 2 1

Contents

Prefatory note

This book is largely intended for students and general readers who are interested in the current state of cultural theory. But I hope it will also prove useful to specialists in the field, not least because it argues against what I take to be a current orthodoxy. I do not believe that this orthodoxy addresses itself to questions searching enough to meet the demands of our political situation, and I try to spell out why this is so and how it might be remedied.

I am grateful to Peter Dews for his illuminating comments on part of the manuscript. The influence of the late Herbert McCabe is so pervasive on my argument that it is impossible to localize.

T.E.
Dublin

I

The Politics of Amnesia

The golden age of cultural theory is long past. The pioneering works of Jacques Lacan, Claude Lévi-Strauss, Louis Althusser, Roland Barthes and Michel Foucault are several decades behind us. So are the path-breaking early writings of Raymond Williams, Luce Irigaray, Pierre Bourdieu, Julia Kristeva, Jacques Derrida, Hélène Cixous, Jurgen Habermas, Fredric Jameson and Edward Said. Not much that has been written since has matched the ambitiousness and originality of these founding mothers and fathers. Some of them have since been struck down. Fate pushed Roland Barthes under a Parisian laundry van, and afflicted Michel Foucault with Aids. It dispatched Lacan, Williams and Bourdieu, and banished Louis Althusser to a psychiatric hospital for the murder of his wife. It seemed that God was not a structuralist.

Many of the ideas of these thinkers remain of incomparable value. Some of them are still producing work of major importance. Those to whom the title of this book suggests that 'theory' is now over, and that we can all relievedly return to an age of pre-theoretical innocence, are in for a disappointment. There can be no going back to an age when it was enough to pronounce Keats delectable or Milton a doughty spirit. It is not as though the whole project was a ghastly mistake on which some merciful soul has now blown the whistle, so that we can all return to whatever it was we were doing before Ferdinand de Saussure heaved over the horizon. If theory means a reasonably systematic reflection on our guiding assumptions, it remains as indispensable as ever. But we are living now in the aftermath of what one might call high theory, in an age which, having grown rich on the insights of thinkers like Althusser, Barthes and Derrida, has also in some ways moved beyond them.

The generation which followed after these path-breaking figures did what generations which follow after usually do. They developed the original ideas, added to them, criticized them and applied them. Those who can, think up feminism or structuralism; those who can't, apply such insights to *Moby-Dick* or *The Cat in the Hat*. But the new generation came up with no comparable body of ideas of its own. The older generation had proved a hard act to follow. No doubt the new century will in time give birth to its own clutch of gurus. For the moment, however, we are still trading on the past – and this in a world which has changed dramatically since Foucault and Lacan first settled to their typewriters. What kind of fresh thinking does the new era demand?

Before we can answer this question, we need to take stock of where we are. Structuralism, Marxism, post-structuralism and the like are no longer the sexy topics they were. What is sexy instead is sex. On the wilder shores of academia, an interest in French philosophy has given way to a fascination with French kissing. In some cultural circles, the politics of masturbation exert far more fascination than the politics of the Middle East. Socialism has lost out to sado-masochism. Among students of culture, the body is an immensely fashionable topic, but it is usually the erotic body, not the famished one. There is a keen interest in coupling bodies, but not in labouring ones. Quietly-spoken middle-class students huddle diligently in libraries, at work on sensationalist subjects like vampirism and eye-gouging, cyborgs and porno movies.

Nothing could be more understandable. To work on the literature of latex or the political implications of navel-piercing is to take literally the wise old adage that study should be fun. It is rather like writing your Master's thesis on the comparative flavour of malt whiskies, or on the phenomenology of lying in bed all day. It creates a seamless continuity between the intellect and everyday life. There are advantages in being able to write your Ph.D. thesis without stirring from in front of the TV set. In the old days, rock music was a distraction from your studies; now it may well be what you are studying. Intellectual matters are no longer an ivory-tower affair, but belong to the world of media and shopping malls, bedrooms and brothels. As such, they re-join everyday life – but only at the risk of losing their ability to subject it to critique.

Today, the old fogeys who work on classical allusions in Milton look askance on the Young Turks who are deep in incest and cyber-feminism. The bright young things who pen essays on foot fetishism or the history of the codpiece eye with suspicion the scrawny old scholars who dare to maintain that Jane Austen is greater than Jeffrey Archer. One zealous orthodoxy gives way to another. Whereas in the old days you could be drummed out of your student drinking club if you failed to spot a metonym in Robert Herrick, you might today be regarded as an unspeakable nerd for having heard of either metonyms or Herrick in the first place.

This trivialization of sexuality is especially ironic. For one of the towering achievements of cultural theory has been to establish gender and sexuality as legitimate objects of study, as well as matters of insistent political importance. It is remarkable how intellectual life for centuries was conducted on the tacit assumption that human beings had no genitals. (Intellectuals also behaved as though men and women lacked stomachs. As the philosopher Emmanuel Levinas remarked of Martin Heidegger's rather lofty concept of *Dasein*, meaning the kind of existence peculiar to human beings: '*Dasein* does not eat.') Friedrich Nietzsche once commented that whenever anybody speaks crudely of a human being as a belly with two needs and a head with one, the lover of knowledge should listen carefully. In an historic advance, sexuality is now firmly established within academic life as one of the keystones of human culture. We have come to acknowledge that human existence is at least as much about fantasy and desire as it is about truth and reason. It is just that cultural theory is at present behaving rather like a celibate middle-aged professor who has stumbled absent-mindedly upon sex and is frenetically making up for lost time.

Another historic gain of cultural theory has been to establish that popular culture is also worth studying. With some honourable exceptions, traditional scholarship has for centuries ignored the everyday life of the common people. Indeed, it was life itself it used to ignore, not just the everyday. In some traditionalist universities not long ago, you could not research on authors who were still alive. This was a great incentive to slip a knife between their ribs one foggy evening, or a remarkable test of patience if your chosen novelist was in rude health and only thirty-four. You certainly could not research on anything you saw around you every day, which was by definition not worth studying. Most things that were deemed suitable for study in the humanities were not visible, like nail-clippings or Jack Nicholson, but invisible, like Stendhal, the concept of sovereignty or the sinuous elegance of Leibniz's notion of the monad. Today it is generally recognized that everyday life is quite as intricate, unfathomable, obscure and occasionally tedious as Wagner, and thus eminently worth investigating. In the old days, the test of what was worth studying was quite often how futile, monotonous and esoteric it was. In some circles today, it is whether it is something you and your friends do in the evenings. Students once wrote uncritical, reverential essays on Flaubert, but all that has been transformed. Nowadays they write uncritical, reverential essays on *Friends*.

Even so, the advent of sexuality and popular culture as kosher subjects of study has put paid to one powerful myth. It has helped to demolish the puritan dogma that seriousness is one thing and pleasure another. The puritan mistakes pleasure for frivolity because he mistakes seriousness for solemnity. Pleasure falls outside the realm of knowledge, and thus is dangerously anarchic. On this view, to *study* pleasure would be like chemically analysing champagne rather than drinking the stuff. The puritan does not see that pleasure and seriousness are related in this sense: that finding out how life can become more pleasant for more people is a serious business. Traditionally, it is known as moral discourse. But 'political' discourse would do just as well.

Yet pleasure, a buzz word for contemporary culture, has its limits too. Finding out how to make life more pleasant is not always pleasant. Like all scientific inquiry, it requires patience, self-discipline and an inexhaustible capacity to be bored. In any case, the hedonist who embraces pleasure as the ultimate reality is often just the puritan in full-throated rebellion. Both of them are usually obsessed with sex. Both of them equate truth with earnestness. Old-style puritanical capitalism forbade us to enjoy ourselves, since once we had acquired a taste for the stuff we would probably never see the inside of the workplace again. Sigmund Freud held that if it were not for what he called the reality principle, we would simply lie around the place all day in various mildly scandalous states of *jouissance*. A more canny, consumerist kind of capitalism, however, persuades us to indulge our senses and gratify ourselves as shamelessly as possible. In that way we will not only consume more goods; we will also identify our own fulfilment with the survival of the system. Anyone who fails to wallow orgasmically in sensual delight will be visited late at night by a terrifying thug known as the superego, whose penalty for such non-enjoyment is atrocious guilt. But since this ruffian also tortures us for having a good time, one might as well take the ha'pence with the kicks and enjoy oneself anyway.

So there is nothing inherently subversive about pleasure. On the contrary, as Karl Marx recognized, it is a thoroughly aristocratic creed. The traditional English gentleman was so averse to unpleasurable labour that he could not even be bothered to articulate properly. Hence the patrician slur and drawl. Aristotle believed that being human was something you had to get good at through constant practice, like learning Catalan or playing the bagpipes; whereas if the English gentleman was virtuous, as he occasionally deigned to be, his goodness was purely spontaneous. Moral effort was for merchants and clerks.

Not all students of culture are blind to the Western narcissism involved in working on the history of pubic hair while half the world's population lacks adequate sanitation and survives on less than two dollars a day. Indeed, the most flourishing sector of cultural studies today is so-called post-colonial studies, which deals with just this dire condition. Like the discourse of gender and sexuality, it has been one of the most precious achievements of cultural theory. Yet these ideas have thrived among new generations who, for no fault of their own, can remember little of world-shaking political importance. Before the advent of the so-called war on terrorism, it seemed as though there might be nothing more momentous for young Europeans to recount to their grandchildren than the advent of the euro. Over the dreary decades of post-1970s conservatism, the historical sense had grown increasingly blunted, as it suited those in power that we should be able to imagine no alternative to the present. The future would simply be the present infinitely repeated – or, as the postmodernist remarked, 'the present plus more options'. There are now those who piously insist on 'historicizing' and who seem to believe that anything that happened before 1980 is ancient history.

To live in interesting times is not, to be sure, an unmixed blessing. It is no particular consolation to be able to recall the Holocaust, or to have lived through the Vietnam war. Innocence and amnesia have their advantages. There is no point in mourning the blissful days when you could have your skull fractured by the police every weekend in Hyde Park. To recall a world-shaking political history is also, for the political left at least, to recall what is for the most part a history of defeat. In any case, a new and ominous phase of global politics has now opened, which not even the most cloistered of academics will be able to ignore. Even so, what has proved most damaging, at least before the emergence of the anti-capitalist movement, is the absence of memories of collective, and effective, political action. It is this which has warped so many contemporary cultural ideas out of shape. There is a historical vortex at the centre of our thought which drags it out of true.

Much of the world as we know it, despite its solid, well-upholstered appearance, is of recent vintage. It was thrown up by the tidal waves of revolutionary nationalism which swept the globe in the period after the Second World War, tearing one nation after another from the grip of Western colonialism. The Allies' struggle in the Second World War was itself a successful collaborative action on a scale unprecedented in human history – one which crushed a malevolent fascism at the heart of Europe, and in doing so laid some of the foundations of the world we know today. Much of the global community we see around us was formed, fairly recently, by collective revolutionary projects – projects which were launched often enough by the weak and hungry, but which nevertheless proved successful in dislodging their predatory foreign rulers. Indeed, the Western empires which those revolutions dismantled were themselves for the most part the product of revolutions. It is just that they were those most victorious revolutions of all – the ones which we have forgotten ever took place. And that usually means the ones which produced the likes of us. Other people's revolutions are always more eye-catching than one's own.

But it is one thing to make a revolution, and another to sustain it. Indeed, for the most eminent revolutionary leader of the twentieth century, what brought some revolutions to birth in the first place was also what was responsible for their ultimate downfall. Vladimir Lenin believed that it was the very backwardness of Tsarist Russia which had helped to make the Bolshevik revolution possible. Russia was a nation poor in the kind of civic institutions which secure the loyalty of citizens to the state, and thus help to stave off political insurrection. Its power was centralized rather than diffuse, coercive rather than consensual: it was concentrated in the state machine, so that to overthrow that was to seize sovereignty at a stroke. But this very same poverty and backwardness helped to scupper the revolution once it had been made. You could not build socialism in an economic back-water, encircled by stronger, politically hostile powers, among a mass of unskilled, illiterate workers and peasants without traditions of social organization and democratic self-government. The attempt to do so called for the strong-armed measures of Stalinism, which ended up subverting the very socialism it was trying to construct.

Something of the same fate afflicted many of those nations who managed in the twentieth century to free themselves from Western colonial rule. In a tragic irony, socialism proved least possible where it was most necessary. Indeed, post-colonial theory first emerged in the wake of the failure of Third World nations to go it alone. It marked the end of the era of Third World revolutions, and the first glimmerings of what we now know as globalization. In the 1950s and 60s, a series of liberation movements, led by the nationalist middle classes, had thrown off their colonial masters in the name of political sovereignty and economic independence. By harnessing the demands of an impoverished people to these goals, the Third World elites could install themselves in power on the back of popular discontent. Once ensconced there, they would need to engage in an ungainly balancing act between radical pressures from below and global market forces from outside.

Marxism, an internationalist current to its core, lent its support to these movements, respecting their demand for political autonomy and seeing in them a grievous setback to world capitalism. But many Marxists harboured few illusions about the aspiring middle-class elites who spearheaded these nationalist currents. Unlike the more sentimental brands of post-colonialism, most Marxism did not assume that 'Third World' meant good and 'First World' bad. They insisted rather on a class-analysis of colonial and post-colonial politics themselves.

Isolated, poverty-stricken and poor in civic, liberal or democratic traditions, some of these regimes found themselves taking the Stalinist path into crippling isolation. Others had to acknowledge that they could not go it alone – that political sovereignty had brought with it no authentic economic self-government, and could never do so in a West-dominated world. As the world capitalist crisis deepened from the early 1970s onwards, and as a number of Third World nations sank further into stagnation and corruption, the aggressive restructurings of a Western capitalism fallen upon hard times finally put paid to illusions of national-revolutionary independence. 'Third Worldism' accordingly gave way to 'post-colonialism'. Edward Said's magisterial *Orientalism*, published in 1978, marked this transition in intellectual terms, despite its author's understandable reservations about much of the post-colonial theory which was to follow in its wake. The book appeared at the turning-point of the fortunes of the international left.

Given the partial failure of national revolution in the so-called Third World, post-colonial theory was wary of all talk of nationhood. Theorists who were either too young or too obtuse to recall that nationalism had been in its time an astonishingly effective anti-colonial force could find in it nothing but a benighted chauvinism or ethnic supremacism. Instead, much post-colonial thought focused on the cosmopolitan dimensions of a world in which post-colonial states were being sucked inexorably into the orbit of global capital. In doing so, it reflected a genuine reality. But in rejecting the idea of nationhood, it also tended to jettison the notion of class, which had been so closely bound up with the revolutionary nation. Most of the new theorists were not only 'post' colonialism, but 'post' the revolutionary impetus which had given birth to the new nations in the first place. If those nation-states had partly failed, unable to get on terms with the affluent capitalist world, then to look beyond the nation seeemed to mean looking beyond class as well – and this at a time when capitalism was more powerful and predatory than ever.

It is true that the revolutionary nationalists had in a sense looked beyond class themselves. By rallying the national people, they could forge a spurious unity out of conflicting class interests.

The middle classes had rather more to gain from national independence than hard-pressed workers and peasants, who would simply find themselves presented with a native rather than a foreign set of exploiters. Even so, this unity was not entirely bogus. If the idea of the nation was a displacement of class conflict, it also served to give it shape. If it fostered some dangerous illusions, it also helped to turn the world upside down. Indeed, revolutionary nationalism was by far the most successful radical tide of the twentieth century. In one sense, different groups and classes in the Third World indeed faced a common Western antagonist. The nation had become the major form which the class struggle against this antagonist had assumed. It was, to be sure, a narrow, distorting form, and in the end would prove woefully inadequate. *The Communist Manifesto* observes that the class struggle first of all takes a national form, but goes well beyond this form in its content. Even so, the nation was a way of rallying different social classes – peasants, workers, students, intellectuals – against the colonial powers which stood in the way of their independence. And it had a powerful argument in its favour: success, at least to begin with.

Some of the new theory, by contrast, saw itself as shifting attention from class to colonialism – as though colonialism and post-colonialism were not themselves matters of class! In its Eurocentric way, it identified class conflict with the West alone, or saw it only in national terms. For socialists, by contrast, anti-colonial struggle was class struggle too: it represented a strike against the power of international capital, which had not been slow to respond to that challenge with sustained military violence. It was a battle between Western capital and the sweated labourers of the world. But because this class conflict had been framed in national terms, it helped to pave the way for the dwindling of the very idea of class in later post-colonial writing. This is one sense in which, as we shall see later, the highpoint of radical ideas in the mid-twentieth century was also the beginning of their downward curve.

Much post-colonial theory shifted the focus from class and nation to ethnicity. This meant among other things that the distinctive problems of post-colonial culture were often falsely assimilated to the very different question of Western 'identity politics'. Since ethnicity is largely a cultural affair, this shift of focus was also one from politics to culture. In some ways, this reflected real changes in the world. But it also helped to depoliticize the question of post-colonialism, and inflate the role of culture within it, in ways which chimed with the new, post-revolutionary climate in the West itself. 'Liberation' was no longer in the air, and by the end of the 1970s 'emancipation' had a quaintly antiquated ring to it. It seemed, then, that having drawn a blank at home, the Western left was now hunting for its stomping ground abroad. In travelling abroad, however, it brought with it in its luggage the burgeoning Western obsession with culture.

Even so, Third World revolutions had testified in their own way to the power of collective action. So in a different way did the militant actions of the Western labour movements, which in the 1970s helped to bring down a British government. So, too, did the peace and student movements of the late 1960s and early 1970s, which played a central part in ending the Vietnam war. Much recent cultural theory, however, has little recollection of all this. From its viewpoint, collective action means launching wars against weaker nations rather than bringing such adventures to a merciful end. In a world which has witnessed the rise and fall of various brutally totalitarian regimes, the whole idea of collective life comes to seem vaguely discredited.

For some postmodern thought, consensus is tyrannical and solidarity nothing but soulless uniformity.[1] But whereas liberals oppose this conformity with the individual, postmodernists, some of whom doubt the very reality of the individual, counter it instead with margins and minorities. It is what stands askew to society as a whole – the marginal, mad, deviant, perverse, transgressive – which is most politically fertile. There can be little value in mainstream social life. And this, ironically, is just the kind of elitist, monolithic viewpoint which postmodernists find most disagreeable in their conservative opponents.

In retrieving what orthodox culture has pushed to the margins, cultural studies has done vital work. Margins can be unspeakably painful places to be, and there are few more honourable tasks for students of culture than to help create a space in which the dumped and disregarded can find a tongue. It is no longer quite so easy to claim that there is nothing to ethnic art but pounding on oil drums or knocking a couple of bones together. Feminism has not only transformed the cultural landscape but, as we shall see later, has become the very model of morality for our time. Meanwhile, those white males who, unfortunately for themselves, are not quite dead have been metaphorically strung upside down from the lamp-posts, while the ill-gotten coins cascading from their pockets have been used to finance community arts projects.

What is under assault here is the *normative*. Majority social life on this view is a matter of norms and conventions, and therefore

1. By 'postmodern', I mean, roughly speaking, the contemporary movement of thought which rejects totalities, universal values, grand historical narratives, solid foundations to human existence and the possibility of objective knowledge. Postmodernism is sceptical of truth, unity and progress, opposes what it sees as elitism in culture, tends towards cultural relativism, and celebrates pluralism, discontinuity and heterogeneity.

inherently oppressive. Only the marginal, perverse and aberrant can escape this dreary regimenting. Norms are oppressive because they mould uniquely different individuals to the same shape. As the poet William Blake writes, 'One Law for the Lion & Ox is oppression.' Liberals accept this normalizing as necessary if everyone is to be granted the same life-chances to fulfil their unique personalities. It will, in short, lead to consequences which undercut it. Libertarians, however, are less resigned to this levelling. In this, they are ironically close to conservatives. Sanguine libertarians like Oscar Wilde dream of a future society in which everyone will be free to be their incomparable selves. For them, there can be no question of weighing and measuring individuals, any more than you could compare the concept of envy with a parrot.

By contrast, pessimistic or shamefaced libertarians like Jacques Derrida and Michel Foucault see that norms are inescapable as soon as we open our mouths. The word 'ketch', which as the reader will know means a two-masted fore-and-aft rigged sailing boat with a mizzen mast stepped forward of the rudder and smaller than its foremast, sounds precise enough, but it has to stretch to cover all sorts of individual crafts of this general kind, each with its own peculiarities. Language levels things down. It is normative all the way down. To say 'leaf' implies that two incomparably different bits of vegetable matter are one and the same. To say 'here' homogenizes all sorts of richly diverse places.

Thinkers like Foucault and Derrida chafe against these equivalences, even if they accept them as unavoidable. They would like a world made entirely out of differences. Indeed, like their great mentor Nietzsche, they think the world *is* made entirely out of differences, but that we need to fashion identities in order to get by. It is true that nobody in a world of pure differences would be able to say anything intelligible – that there could be no poetry, road signs, love letters or log sheets, as well as no statements that everything is uniquely different from everything else. But this is simply the price one would have to pay for not being constrained by the behaviour of others, like paying that little bit extra for a first-class rail ticket.

It is a mistake, however, to believe that norms are always restrictive. In fact it is a crass Romantic delusion. It is normative in our kind of society that people do not throw themselves with a hoarse cry on total strangers and amputate their legs. It is conventional that child murderers are punished, that working men and women may withdraw their labour, and that ambulances speeding to a traffic accident should not be impeded just for the hell of it. Anyone who feels oppressed by all this must be seriously oversensitive. Only an intellectual who has overdosed on abstraction could be dim enough to imagine that whatever bends a norm is politically radical.

Those who believe that normativity is always negative are also likely to hold that authority is always suspect. In this, they differ from radicals, who respect the authority of those with long experience of fighting injustice, or of laws which safeguard people's physical integrity or working conditions. Similarly, some modern-day cultural thinkers seem to believe that minorities are always more vibrant than majorities. It is not the most popular of beliefs among the disfigured victims of Basque separatism. Some fascist groups, however, may be flattered to hear it, along with UFO buffs and Seventh Day Adventists. It was majorities, not minorities, which confounded imperial power in India and brought down apartheid. Those who oppose norms, authority and majorities as such are abstract universalists, even though most of them oppose abstract universalism as well.

The postmodern prejudice against norms, unities and consensuses is a politically catastrophic one. It is also remarkably dim-witted. But it does not only spring from having precious few examples of political solidarity to remember. It also reflects a real social change. It is one result of the apparent disintegration of old-fashioned bourgeois society into a host of sub-cultures. One of the historic developments of our age has been the decline of the traditional middle class. As Perry Anderson has argued, the solid, civilized, morally upright bourgeoisie which managed to survive the Second World War has given way in our time to 'starlet princesses and sleazeball presidents, beds for rent in the official residence and bribes for killer ads, disneyfication of protocols and tarantinization of practices'. The 'solid (bourgeois) amphitheatre', Anderson writes with colourful contempt, has yielded to 'an aquarium of floating, evanescent forms – the projectors and managers, auditors and janitors, administrators and speculators of contemporary capital: functions of a monetary universe that knows no social fixities and stable identities'.[2] It is this lack of stable identities which for some cultural theory today is the last word in radicalism. Instability of identity is 'subversive' – a claim which it would be interesting to test out among the socially dumped and disregarded.

In this social order, then, you can no longer have bohemian rebels or revolutionary avant-gardes because they no longer have anything to blow up. Their top-hatted, frock-coated, easily outraged enemy has evaporated. Instead, the non-normative has become the norm. Nowadays, it is not just anarchists for whom anything goes, but starlets, newspaper editors, stockbrokers and corporation executives. The norm now is money; but since money has absolutely no principles or identity of its own, it is no kind of

2. Perry Anderson, *The Origins of Postmodernity*, London, 1998, pp. 86 and 85.

norm at all. It is utterly promiscuous, and will happily tag along with the highest bidder. It is infinitely adaptive to the most bizarre or extremist of situations, and like the Queen has no opinions of its own about anything.

It seems, then, as though we have moved from the high-minded hypocrisy of the old middle classes to the low-minded effrontery of the new ones. We have shifted from a national culture with a single set of rules to a motley assortment of sub-cultures, each one at an angle to the others. This, of course, is an exaggeration. The old regime was never as unified as that, nor the new one as fragmented. There are still some powerful collective norms at work in it. But it is true, by and large, that our new ruling elite consists increasingly of people who snort cocaine rather than people who look like Herbert Asquith or Marcel Proust.

The current of cultural experiment we know as modernism was fortunate in this respect. Rimbaud, Picasso and Bertolt Brecht still had a classical bourgeoisie to be rude about. But its offspring, postmodernism, has not. It is just that it seems not to have noticed the fact, perhaps because it is too embarrassing to acknowledge. Postmodernism seems at times to behave as though the classical bourgeoisie is alive and well, and thus finds itself living in the past. It spends much of its time assailing absolute truth, objectivity, timeless moral values, scientific inquiry and a belief in historical progress. It calls into question the autonomy of the individual, inflexible social and sexual norms, and the belief that there are firm foundations to the world. Since all of these values belong to a bourgeois world on the wane, this is rather like firing off irascible letters to the press about the horse-riding Huns or marauding Carthaginians who have taken over the Home Counties.

This is not to say that these beliefs do not still have force. In places like Ulster and Utah, they are riding high. But nobody on Wall Street and few in Fleet Street believe in absolute truth and unimpeachable foundations. A lot of scientists are fairly sceptical about science, seeing it as much more of a hit-and-miss, rule-of-thumb affair than the gullible layperson imagines. It is people in the humanities who still naïvely think that scientists consider themselves the white-coated custodians of absolute truth, and so waste a lot of time trying to discredit them. Humanists have always been sniffy about scientists. It is just that they used to despise them for snobbish reasons, and now do so for sceptical ones. Few of the people who believe in absolute moral values in theory do so in practice. They are known mainly as politicians and business executives. Conversely, some of the people who might be expected to believe in absolute values believe in nothing of the kind, like moral philosophers and clap-happy clerics. And though some genetically upbeat Americans may still have faith in progress, a huge number of constitutionally downbeat Europeans do not.

But it is not only the traditional middle class which has faded from view. It is also the traditional working class. And since the working class stood for political solidarity, it is scarcely surprising that we should now have a form of radicalism which is deeply distrustful of all that. Postmodernism does not believe in individualism, since it does not believe in individuals; but it does not pin much faith in working-class community either. Instead, it puts its trust in pluralism – in a social order which is as diverse and inclusive as possible. The problem with this as a radical case is that there is not much in it with which Prince Charles would disagree. It is true that capitalism quite often creates divisions and exclusions for its own purposes. Either that, or it draws upon ones which already exist. And these exclusions can be profoundly hurtful for a great many people. Whole masses of men and women have suffered the misery and indignity of second-class citizenship. In principle, however, capitalism is an impeccably inclusive creed: it really doesn't care who it exploits. It is admirably egalitarian in its readiness to do down just about anyone. It is prepared to rub shoulders with any old victim, however unappetizing. Most of the time, at least, it is eager to mix together as many diverse cultures as possible, so that it can peddle its commodities to them all.

In the generously humanistic spirit of the ancient poet, this system regards nothing human as alien to it. In its hunt for profit, it will travel any distance, endure any hardship, shack up with the most obnoxious of companions, suffer the most abominable humiliations, tolerate the most tasteless wallpaper and cheerfully betray its next of kin. It is capitalism which is disinterested, not dons. When it comes to consumers who wear turbans and those who do not, those who sport flamboyant crimson waistcoats and those who wear nothing but a loincloth, it is sublimely even-handed. It has the scorn for hierarchies of a truculent adolescent, and the zeal to pick and mix of an American diner. It thrives on bursting bounds and slaying sacred cows. Its desire is unslakeable and its space infinite. Its law is the flouting of all limits, which makes law indistinguishable from criminality. In its sublime ambition and extravagant transgressions, it makes its most shaggily anarchic critics look staid and suburban.

There are other, familiar problems with the idea of inclusiveness, which need not detain us too long. Who gets to decide who gets included? Who – the Groucho Marx query – would want to be included in this set-up anyway? If marginality is as fertile, subversive a place as postmodern thinkers tend to suggest, why would they want to abolish it? Anyway, what if there is no clear division between margins and majority? For a socialist, the true scandal of the present world is that almost everyone in it is banished to the margins. As far as the transnational corporations go, great masses of men and women are really neither here nor there. Whole nations are thrust to the periphery. Entire classes of people are deemed to be dysfunctional. Communities are uprooted and forced into migration.

In this world, what is central can alter overnight: nothing and nobody is permanently indispensable, least of all corporation executives. Who or what is key to the system is debatable. The destitute are obviously marginal, as so much debris and detritus thrown up by the global economy; but what of the low-paid? The low-paid are not central, but neither are they marginal. It is they whose labour keeps the system up and running. And on a global scale, the low-paid means an enormous mass of people. This, curiously, is a set-up which shuts out most of its members. And in that it is like any class-society which has ever existed. Or, for that matter, like patriarchal society, which disadvantages roughly half of its members.

As long as we think of margins as *minorities*, this extraordinary fact is conveniently obscured. Most cultural thinking these days comes from the United States, a country which houses some sizeable ethnic minorities as well as most of the world's great corporations. But because Americans are not much used to thinking in international terms, given that their governments are more interested in ruling the world than reflecting upon it, 'marginal' comes to mean Mexican or African-American, rather than, in addition, the people of Bangladesh or the former coalminers and shipbuilders of the West. Coalminers don't seem all that Other, except in the eyes of a few of D. H. Lawrence's characters.

Indeed, there are times when it does not seem to matter all that much who the Other is. It is just any group who will show you up in your dismal normativity. A murky subcurrent of masochism runs beneath this exoticizing, laced with a dash of good old-fashioned American puritan guilt. If you were white and Western, it was better to be more or less anyone but yourself. The felicitous unearthing of a Manx great-grandmother or serendipitous stumbling across a Cornish second cousin might go some way towards assuaging your guilt. With an arrogance thinly masked as humility, the cult of the Other assumes that there are no major conflicts or contradictions within the social majority themselves. Or, for that matter, within the minorities. There is just Them and Us, margins and majorities. Some of the people who hold this view are also deeply suspicious of binary oppositions.

There can be no falling back on ideas of collectivity which belong to a world unravelling before our eyes. Human history is now for the most part both post-collectivist and post-individualist; and if this feels like a vacuum, it may also present an opportunity. We need to imagine new forms of belonging, which in our kind of world are bound to be multiple rather than monolithic. Some of those forms will have something of the intimacy of tribal or community relations, while others will be more abstract, mediated and indirect. There is no single ideal size of society to belong to, no Cinderella's slipper of a space. The ideal size of community used to be known as the nation-state, but even some nationalists no longer see this as the only desirable terrain.

If men and women need freedom and mobility, they also need a sense of tradition and belonging. There is nothing retrograde about roots. The postmodern cult of the migrant, which sometimes succeeds in making migrants sound even more enviable than rock stars, is a good deal too supercilious in this respect. It is a hangover from the modernist cult of the exile, the Satanic artist who scorns the suburban masses and plucks an elitist virtue out of his enforced dispossession. The problem at the moment is that the rich have mobility while the poor have locality. Or rather, the poor have locality until the rich get their hands on it. The rich are global and the poor are local – though just as poverty is a global fact, so the rich are coming to appreciate the benefits of locality. It is not hard to imagine affluent communities of the future protected by watchtowers, searchlights and machine-guns, while the poor scavenge for food in the waste lands beyond. In the meantime, rather more encouragingly, the anti-capitalist movement is seeking to sketch out new relations between globality and locality, diversity and solidarity.

2

The Rise and Fall of Theory

Cultural ideas change with the world they reflect upon. If they insist, as they do, on the need to see things in their historical context, then this must also apply to themselves. Even the most rarefied theories have a root in historical reality. Take, for example, hermeneutics, the science or art of interpretation. It is generally agreed that the founding father of hermeneutics was the German philosopher Friedrich Schleiermacher. What is not so widely known is that Schleiermacher's interest in the art of interpretation was provoked when he was invited to translate a book entitled *An Account of the English Colony in New South Wales*, which records the author's encounter with Australian Aboriginal peoples. Schleiermacher was concerned about how we could understand the beliefs of this people even though they seemed desperately alien to us.[1] It was from a colonial encounter that the art of interpretation was born.

Cultural theory must be able to give some account of its own historical rise, flourishing and faltering. Strictly speaking, such theory goes back as far as Plato. In the forms most familiar to us, however, it is really a product of an extraordinary decade

1. See Andrew Bowie (ed.), *Friedrich Schleiermacher: Hermeneutics and Criticism*, Cambridge, 1998, p. xix.

and a half, from about 1965 to 1980. It is in this astonishingly abundant period that most of the thinkers listed at the opening of the previous chapter produced their path-breaking works.

What is the significance of these dates? It is that cultural theory broke out in the only period since the Second World War in which the political far left rose briefly to prominence, before sinking almost out of sight. The new cultural ideas had their roots deep in the age of civil rights and student insurgency, national liberation fronts, anti-war and anti-nuclear campaigns, the emergence of the women's movement and the heyday of cultural liberation. It was an era in which the consumer society was launched with a flourish; in which the media, popular culture, sub-cultures and the cult of youth first emerged as social forces to be reckoned with; and in which social hierarchies and traditional mores were coming under satiric assault. The whole sensibility of society had undergone one of its periodic transformations. We had shifted from the earnest, self-disciplined and submissive to the cool, hedonistic and insubordinate. If there was widespread disaffection, there was also visionary hope. There was a general excited sense that the present was the place to be. And if it was, it was partly because it seemed so obviously the herald of a new future, the portal to a land of boundless possibility.

Above all, the new cultural ideas sprang up in a capitalism for which culture itself was becoming more and more important. This was an unusual development. Culture and capitalism are hardly as familiar a duo as Corneille and Racine or Laurel and Hardy. Indeed, culture had traditionally signified almost the opposite of capitalism. The concept of culture grew up as a critique of middle-class society, not as an ally of it. Culture was about values rather than prices, the moral rather than the material, the high-minded rather than the philistine. It was about the cultivation of human powers as ends in themselves rather than for some ignobly utilitarian motive. Such powers formed a harmonious totality: they were not just a bundle of specialized tools, and 'culture' signified this splendid synthesis. It was the rickety shelter where the values and energies which industrial capitalism had no use for could take refuge. It was the place where the erotic and symbolic, the ethical and mythological, the sensuous and affective, could set up home in a social order which had less and less time for any of them. From its patrician height, it scorned the shopkeepers and stockbrokers swarming in the commercial badlands below.

By the 1960s and 70s, however, culture was also coming to mean film, image, fashion, lifestyle, marketing, advertising, the communications media. Signs and spectacles were spreading throughout social life. There were anxieties in Europe about cultural Americanization. We seemed to have achieved affluence without fulfilment, which brought cultural or 'quality of life' issues sharply to the fore. Culture in the sense of value, symbol, language, art, tradition and identity was the very air which new social movements like feminism and Black Power breathed. It was now on the side of dissent, not of harmonious resolution. It was also the life-blood of newly articulate working-class artists and critics, who were noisily besieging the bastions of high culture and higher education for the first time. The idea of cultural revolution migrated from the so-called Third World to the well-heeled West, in a heady *mélange* of Fanon, Marcuse, Reich, Beauvoir, Gramsci and Godard.

Meanwhile, a conflict broke out on the streets over the uses of knowledge. It was a quarrel between those who wanted to turn knowledge into military and technological hardware, or into techniques of administrative control, and those who saw in it a chance for political emancipation. The universities which had been the very home of traditional culture, the citadels of disinterested inquiry, became for a fleeting moment, most unusually, the cockpits of culture as political struggle. Middle-class society had been reckless enough to set up institutions in which young, clever, morally conscientious people had nothing to do for three or four years but read books and kick ideas around; and the result of this ludicrous indulgence on society's part was wholesale student revolt. Nor was it confined to the campus, like today's campaigns for political correctness. In France and Italy, student agitation helped to detonate the largest mass working-class protests of the post-war era.

This, to be sure, is only likely to come about in peculiar political circumstances. In our own time, political conflict on the campuses has been largely about words rather than red bases. Indeed, the former is partly a result of the disappearance of the latter. Even so, allowing sensitive, politically idealistic young people to gather together for several years on end remains an imprudent policy. There is always a risk that education may put you at odds with the tasteless, clueless philistines who run the world and whose lexicon stretches only to words like oil, golf, power and cheeseburger. It may make you less than sanguine about entrusting the governance of the globe to men who have never been excited by an idea, moved by a landscape or enthralled by the transcendent elegance of a mathematical solution. You may develop grave doubts about those who have the nerve to speak of defending civilization and would not recognize an obelisk or an oboe concerto if it were to slap them in the face. These are the men and women who prate of freedom and would recognize it only in the form of a hand-out.

Some of the political struggles of this period were reasonably successful, while others were not. The student movement of the late 1960s did not prevent higher education from becoming locked ever deeper into structures of military violence and industrial exploitation. But it posed a challenge to the way in which the humanities had been complicit in all this; and one of the fruits of this challenge was cultural theory. The humanities had lost their innocence: they could no longer pretend to be untainted by power. If they wanted to stay in business, it was now vital that they paused to reflect on their own purposes and assumptions. It is this critical self-reflection which we know as theory. Theory of this kind comes about when we are forced into a new self-consciousness about what we are doing. It is a symptom of the fact that we can no longer take those practices for granted. On the contrary, those practices must now begin to take themselves as objects of their own inquiry. There is thus always something rather navel-staring and narcissistic about theory, as anyone who has encountered a few prominent cultural theorists will be aware.

Elsewhere, the record was fairly chequered. If colonial powers were cast out, neo-colonial ones were being levered into their place. For all the climate of post-war affluence, there were still important mass Communist parties in Europe. But they responded at best churlishly and at worst repressively to the stirring of the new social forces. By the 1970s, with the emergence of so-called Eurocommunism, they had opted more decisively than ever for reformism over revolutionism. The women's movement chalked up some signal achievements, suffered some serious rebuffs, and altered much of the cultural climate of the West almost beyond recognition.

Something of the same can be said for the various campaigns for civil rights. In Northern Ireland, the dictatorship of the Unionists was besieged by mass protest, but whether there will be a wholly democratic outcome still remains to be seen. The Western peace movement helped to halt Lyndon Johnson in his bellicose tracks, but failed to abolish weapons of mass destruction. In playing its part in ending the war in south-east Asia, it also did itself out of business as a mass political movement. Elsewhere in the world, however, revolutionary currents continued to upturn colonial powers.

As far as culture goes, the bland, paternalist cultural establishment of the post-war epoch was rudely shattered by the populist experiments of the 1960s. Elitism was now a thought-crime only slightly less grievous than anti-Semitism. Everywhere one looked, the upper middle classes were assiduously at work roughening up their accents and distressing their jeans. The working-class hero was triumphantly marketed. Yet this politically rebellious populism also paved the way for the rampantly consumerist culture of the 1980s and 90s. What had for a moment shaken middle-class complacency was soon to be co-opted by it. Similarly, managers of shops and pubs did not know whether to be enthralled or appalled by Sixties slogans like 'What do we want? Everything! When do we want it? Now!' Capitalism needs a human being who has never yet existed – one who is prudently restrained in the office and wildly anarchic in the shopping mall. What was happening in the 1960s was that the disciplines of production were being challenged by the culture of consumption. And this was bad news for the system only in a limited sense.

There was no simple rise and fall of radical ideas. We have seen already that revolutionary nationalism chalked up some signal victories at the same time that it unwittingly prepared the ground for a 'post-class' discourse of the impoverished world. While students were discovering free love, a brutal US imperialism was at its height in south-east Asia. If there were fresh demands for liberation, they were partly reactions to a capitalism in buoyant, expansive phase. It was the soullessness of an affluent society, not the harshness of a deprived one, which was under fire. European Communist parties made some inroads, but political reform in Czechoslovakia was crushed by Soviet tanks. Latin American guerrilla movements were rolled back. Structuralism, the new intellectual fashion, was radical in some ways and technocratic in others. If it challenged the prevailing social order, it also reflected it. Post-structuralism and postmodernism were to prove similarly ambiguous, subverting the metaphysical underpinnings of middle-class society with something of its own market-type relativism. Both postmodernists and neo-liberals are suspicious of public norms, inherent values, given hierarchies, authoritative standards, consensual codes and traditional practices. It is just that neo-liberals admit that they reject all this in the name of the market. Radical postmodernists, by contrast, combine these aversions with a somewhat sheepish chariness of commercialism. The neo-liberals, at least, have the virtue of consistency here, whatever their plentiful vices elsewhere.

The early 1970s – the very highpoint of radical dissent – also saw the first glimmerings of the postmodern culture which was eventually to take over from it. The halcyon days of cultural theory lasted until about 1980 – several years after the oil crisis which heralded a global recession, the victory of the radical right and the ebbing of revolutionary hopes. Working-class militancy, having flourished in the early 1970s, subsided dramatically, as a systematic onslaught was launched on the labour movement with the aim of breaking it for ever. Trade unions were shackled and unemployment deliberately created. Theory overshot reality, in a kind of intellectual backwash to a tumultuous political era. As often happens, ideas had a last, brilliant efflorescence when the conditions which produced them were already disappearing. Cultural theory was cut loose from its moment of origin, yet tried in its way to keep that moment warm. Like war, it became the continuation of politics by other means. The emancipation which had failed in the streets and factories could be acted out instead in erotic intensities or the floating signifier. Discourse and desire came to stand in for the Godard and Guevara that had failed. At the same time, some of the new ideas were the first straws in the wind of post-political pessimism which was about to blow through the West.

The record was mixed in another sense too. New theories of discourse, deviancy and desire were not simply alternatives to a political leftism that had failed. They were also ways of deepening and enriching it. Perhaps, so some argued, it would not have failed in the first place had it taken these insights fully on board. Cultural theory was there to remind the traditional left of what it had flouted: art, pleasure, gender, power, sexuality, language, madness, desire, spirituality, the family, the body, the ecosystem, the unconscious, ethnicity, life-style, hegemony. This, on any estimate, was a sizeable slice of human existence. One needed to be pretty myopic to overlook as much as this. It was rather like an account of human anatomy which left out the lungs and stomach. Or like the medieval Irish monk who wrote a dictionary but unaccountably omitted the letter S.

In fact, traditional left politics – which at the time really meant Marxism – was never quite as purblind as this suggests. It had had a great deal to say of art and culture, some of it tedious, some of it arrestingly original. In fact, culture bulked large in the tradition which has come to be known as Western Marxism. Georg Lukács, Walter Benjamin, Antonio Gramsci, Wilhelm Reich, Max Horkheimer, Herbert Marcuse, Theodor Adorno, Ernst Bloch, Lucien Goldmann, Jean-Paul Sartre, Fredric Jameson: these are hardly thinkers who ignored the erotic and symbolic, art and the unconscious, lived experience and transformations of consciousness. There is arguably no richer heritage of such thought in the twentieth century. It was from this heritage that modern-day cultural studies took its cue, though much of it is a pale shadow of its predecessors.

Western Marxism's shift to culture was born partly out of political impotence and disenchantment. Caught between capitalism and Stalinism, groups like the Frankfurt School could compensate for their political homelessness by turning to cultural and philosophical questions. Politically marooned, they could draw upon their formidable cultural resources to confront a capitalism in which the role of culture was becoming more and more vital, and thus prove themselves once more politically relevant. In the same act, they could dissociate themselves from a savagely philistine Communist world, while immeasurably enriching the traditions of thought that Communism had betrayed. In doing so, however, much Western Marxism ended up as a somewhat gentrified version of its militant revolutionary forebears, academicist, disillusioned and politically toothless. This, too, it passed on to its successors in cultural studies, for whom such thinkers as Antonio Gramsci came to mean theories of subjectivity rather than workers' revolution.

Marxism had certainly sidelined gender and sexuality. But it had by no means ignored these topics, even though much of what it had to say about them was painfully insufficient. The uprising which was to topple the Russian Tsar and install a Bolshevik regime in his place was launched with demonstrations on International Women's Day in 1917. Once in power, the Bolsheviks gave equality for women a high priority. Marxism had been largely silent on the environment, but so at the time had almost everyone else. There were, even so, some pregnant reflections on Nature in the early Marx and later socialist thinkers. Marxism had not exactly overlooked the unconscious, simply dismissed it out of hand as a bourgeois invention. Yet there were important exceptions to this simple-mindedness, like the Marxist psychoanalyst Wilhelm Reich; and pleasure and desire had played a key role in the reflections of Marxist philosophers like Herbert

31

Marcuse. One of the finest books ever written on the body, *The Phenomenology of Perception*, was the work of the French leftist Maurice Merleau-Ponty. It was through the influence of phenomenology that some Marxist thinkers came to engage with questions of lived experience and everyday life.

The charge that Marxism has had nothing to say about race, nation, colonialism or ethnicity is equally false. Indeed, the Communist movement was the only place in the early twentieth century where the issues of nationalism and colonialism – along with the question of gender – were systematically raised and debated. As Robert J. C. Young has written: 'Communism was the first, and only, political programme to recognize the inter-relation of these different forms of domination and exploitation (class, gender and colonialism) and the necessity of abolishing all of them as the fundamental basis for the successful realization of the liberation of each.'[2] Lenin put colonial revolution at the forefront of the priorities of the Soviet government. Marxist ideas became vital to anti-colonial struggles in India, Africa, Latin America and elsewhere.

In fact, Marxism was the primary inspiration behind anti-colonial campaigns. Many of the great anti-colonial theorists and political leaders of the twentieth century were educated in the West, and learned enduringly from Western Marxism. Gandhi drew on Ruskin, Tolstoy and other such sources. Most Marxist states have been non-European. It is arguable that cultural politics themselves, as the West knows them, were for the most part the product of so-called Third World thinkers like Castro, Cabral, Fanon and James Connolly. Some postmodern

2. Robert J. C. Young, *Postcolonialism: An Historical Introduction*, Oxford, 2001, p. 142. I am indebted to this excellent study for several of the points made here.

thinkers would doubtless regard it as a pity that 'Third World' militants should have had recourse to such manifestations of dominative Western Reason as Marxism. These are the kind of theorists who would point out that, say, the Marquis de Condorcet, a leading figure of the French Enlightenment, believed to his discredit in disinterested knowledge, the splendours of science, perpetual progress, abstract human rights, the infinite perfectibility of humankind, and the steady unfolding in history of the essence of true humanity.

Condorcet certainly held such views. It is just that the same theorists, carried away by their entirely understandable disapproval of these opinions, might well forget to point out that he also believed – at a time when precious few others did – in universal suffrage, equal rights for women, non-violent political revolution, equal education for all, the welfare state, colonial emancipation, free speech, religious tolerance and the overthrow of both despotism and clericalism. These humane views were not at all unrelated to his unprepossessing philosophy, though they can be detached from it. Enlightenment is, one might claim, as Enlightenment does. There are those today for whom 'teleology', 'progress' and 'universalism' are such heinous thought-crimes (which, indeed, they have sometimes most certainly proved to be) that they entirely overshadow a little matter like being a couple of centuries ahead of one's time in practical political terms.

It is true, even so, that the Communist movement had been culpably silent on some central questions. But Marxism is not some Philosophy of Life or Secret of the Universe, which feels duty bound to pronounce on everything from how to break your way into a boiled egg to the quickest way to delouse cocker spaniels. It is an account, roughly speaking, of how one historical mode of production changes into another. It is not a deficiency of Marxism that it has nothing very interesting to say about whether physical exercise or wiring your jaws together is the best way of dieting. Nor is it a defect of feminism that it has so far remained silent about the Bermuda Triangle. Some of those who upbraid Marxism with not saying enough are also allergic to grand narratives which try to say too much.

A lot of the cultural theory which emerged in the 1960s and 70s can be seen as a critique of classical Marxism. On the whole, it was a comradely rather than hostile response – a situation which was later to change. Marxism, for example, had been the guiding theoretical light of the new revolutionary nationalist movements in Asia and Africa; but this, inevitably, had meant a remaking of the theory to meet distinctively new conditions, not the obedient application of a given body of knowledge. From Kenya to Malaysia, revolutionary nationalism had both revived Marxism and forced it to rethink itself. There was also a heated, highly productive debate between Marxists and feminists. Louis Althusser was a Marxist who felt the need to dismantle many received Marxist ideas. Claude Lévi-Strauss was a Marxist who felt Marxism could contribute little to his special field of expertise, anthropology. As an historical outlook, it seemed to throw little light on pre-historic culture and mythology.

Roland Barthes was a man of the left who found Marxism lamentably lacking when it came to semiotics, the science of signs. Julia Kristeva worked on language, desire and the body, none of which had exactly headed the Marxist agenda. Yet both thinkers had close affinities at this point to Marxist politics. The postmodern philosopher Jean-François Lyotard found Marxism irrelevant to information theory and the artistic avant-garde. The most avant-garde cultural journal of the period, the French literary organ *Tel Quel*, discovered an ephemeral alternative to Stalinism in Maoism. This was rather like finding an alternative to heroin in crack cocaine. New connections were forged between

Paris and the paddyfields. Many others found an alternative in Trotskyism.

The litany can be extended. Jacques Derrida claims nowadays that he has always understood his own theory of deconstruction as a kind of radicalized Marxism. Whether this is true or not, deconstruction acted for a while as a kind of code for anti-Communist dissent in some intellectual circles in Eastern Europe. Michel Foucault, a student of Louis Althusser, was a post-Marxist heretic who found Marxism unpersuasive on questions of power, madness and sexuality, but who continued to move for a while within its general ambience. Marxism provided Foucault with a silent interlocutor in several of his most renowned works. The French sociologist Henri Lefebvre found classical Marxism bereft of a notion of everyday life, a concept which in his hands was to exert a potent influence on the militants of 1968. The sociologist Pierre Bourdieu plundered the resources of Marxist theory to produce such concepts as 'symbolic capital', while remaining distinctly sceptical of Marxism as a whole. There were times when it was well-nigh impossible to tell whether the finest cultural thinker of post-war Britain, Raymond Williams, was a Marxist or not. But this was more a strength of his work than a fatal ambiguity. The same goes for much of the so-called New Left, in Britain and the USA. The new cultural thinkers were fellow-travellers – but fellow-travellers of Marxism rather than of Soviet Communism, unlike their predecessors in the 1930s.

Not all of the new cultural thinkers had this fraught relationship with Marxist ideas. But it seems fair to say that much of the new cultural theory was born out of an extraordinarily creative dialogue with Marxism. It began as an attempt to find a way around Marxism without quite leaving it behind. It ended by doing exactly that. In France, the dialogue repeated in a different key an earlier *rapprochement* between Marxism, humanism and existentialism, centred on the revered figure of Jean-Paul Sartre. Sartre once famously observed that Marxism represented a kind of ultimate horizon for the twentieth century, which one could ignore but not go beyond. Thinkers like Foucault and Kristeva, however, were now busy going beyond it – but it was *this* horizon they were striving to surpass, not some other. Nobody was quarrelling with Taoism or Duns Scotus. To this extent, if only negatively, Marxism retained its centrality. It was the thing to bounce off against. If the new cultural thinkers could be sharply critical of it, some of them still shared something of its radical vision. They were, at the very least, Communists in the sense that John F. Kennedy was a Berliner.

In fact, it was sometimes hard to say whether these theorists were repudiating Marxism or renewing it. To do so, you would need to have a fairly exact idea of what Marxism was in the first place. But had this not been precisely part of the trouble? Was this not one reason why Marxism had won itself such a bad name? Was it not presumptuous to suppose that there was a strict definition of the theory, against which you could measure other versions of it for their degrees of criminal deviancy? It was rather like the old argument about whether Freudianism was a science. Both sides of the quarrel seemed to take for granted exactly what science was; the only question was whether Freudianism fitted into it. But what if psychoanalysis forced us to overhaul our idea of what counted as science in the first place?

What mattered, surely, were your politics, not how you pigeon-holed them. Of course there has to be *something* specific to a particular body of ideas. At the very least, there has to be something which counts as incompatible with it. You could not be a Marxist and clamour for a return to slavery. Feminism is a fairly loose collection of beliefs, but however loose it is it cannot include worshipping men as a superior species. It is true that there are some Anglican clerics who seem to reject God, Jesus, the virgin birth, miracles, the resurrection, hell, heaven, the real presence and original sin, but this is because, being gentle, infinitely accepting souls, they do not like to offend anybody by believing anything too uncomfortably specific. They just believe that everybody should be nice to each other. But the alternative to dogmatism is not the assumption that anything goes.

In some quarters, however, Marxism had become just such a species of dogmatism, not least under Stalin and his successors. In the name of Marxism, millions had been slaughtered, persecuted and imprisoned. The question was whether you could loosen the theory up without it falling apart. The answer of some of the cultural pioneers was a guarded yes; the answer of the postmodernists is an unequivocal no. Before long, as Eastern Europe continued on its downhill slope to disaster, most of the pioneers would come round to this conclusion themselves. Just as the radical cultural populism of the 1960s was to pave the way, despite itself, for the cynical consumerism of the 80s, so some of the cultural theory of the time set out to radicalize Marxism, and ended often enough by moving beyond politics altogether. It started out by deepening Marxism, and ended up by displacing it. Julia Kristeva and the *Tel Quel* group turned to religious mysticism and a celebration of the American way of life. Post-structuralist pluralism now seemed best exemplified not by the Chinese cultural revolution but by the North American supermarket. Roland Barthes shifted from politics to pleasure. Jean-François Lyotard turned his attention to intergalactic travel and supported the right-wing Giscard in the French presidential elections. Michel Foucault renounced all aspirations to a new social order. If Louis Althusser rewrote Marxism from the inside, he opened a door in doing so through which many of his disciples would shuffle out of it altogether.

So the crisis of Marxism did not begin with the crumbling of the Berlin wall. It could be felt at the very heart of the political radicalism of the late 60s and early 70s. Not only that, but it was to a large extent the driving force behind the cascade of provocative new ideas. When Lyotard rejected what he called grand narratives, he first used the term to mean, simply, Marxism. The Soviet invasion of Czechoslovakia occurred at the same moment as the celebrated student uprising of 1968. If carnival was in the air, so was the Cold War. It was not a question of the left first flourishing and then declining. As far as classical Marxism went, the worm was already in the bud, the serpent curled secretly in the garden.

Marxism had been badly tarnished in the West by the monstrosities of Stalinism. But many felt that it had also been discredited by changes in capitalism itself. It seemed ill-adapted to a new kind of capitalist system which revolved on consumption rather than production, image rather than reality, the media rather than cotton mills. Above all, it seemed ill-adapted to affluence. The post-war economic boom may have been on its last legs by the late 1960s, but it was still setting the political pace. Many of the problems which preoccupied militant students and radical theorists in the West were ones bred by progress, not poverty. They were problems of bureaucratic regulation, conspicuous consumption, sophisticated military hardware, technologies which seemed to be lurching out of control. The sense of a world which was claustrophobically coded, administered, shot through with signs and conventions from end to end, helped to give birth to structuralism, which investigates the hidden codes and conventions which produce human meaning. The 1960s were stifling as well as swinging. There were anxieties about packaged learning, advertising and the despotic power of the commodity. Some years later, the cultural theory which examined all this would itself be at risk of becoming one more glossy commodity, a way of touting one's symbolic capital. These were all questions of culture, lived experience, utopian desire, the emotional and perceptual damage wrought by a two-dimensional society. They were not matters which Marxism had traditionally had much to say about.

Pleasure, desire, art, language, the media, the body, gender, ethnicity: a single word to sum all these up would be *culture*. Culture, in a sense of the word which included Bill Wyman and fast food as well as Debussy and Dostoevsky, was what Marxism seemed to be lacking. And this is one reason why the dialogue with Marxism was pitched largely on that terrain. Culture was also a way for the civilized, humanistic left to distance itself from the crass philistinism of actually existing socialism. Nor was it surprising that it was cultural theory, rather than politics, economics or orthodox philosophy, which took issue with Marxism in those turbulent years. Students of culture quite often tend to be politically radical, if not easily disciplined. Because subjects like literature and art history have no obvious material pay-off, they tend to attract those who look askance at capitalist notions of utility. The idea of doing something purely for the delight of it has always rattled the grey-bearded guardians of the state. Sheer pointlessness is a deeply subversive affair.

In any case, art and literature encompass a great many ideas and experiences which are hard to reconcile with the present political set-up. They also raise questions of the quality of life in a world where experience itself seems brittle and degraded. How in such conditions can you produce worthwhile art in the first place? Would you not need to change society in order to flourish as an artist? Besides, those who deal with art speak the language of value rather than price. They deal with works whose depth and intensity show up the meagreness of everyday life in a market-obsessed society. They are also trained to imagine alternatives to the actual. Art encourages you to fantasize and desire. For all these reasons, it is easy to see why it is students of art or English rather than chemical engineering who tend to staff the barricades.

Students of chemical engineering, however, are in general better at getting out of bed than students of art and English. Some of the very qualities which attract cultural specialists to the political left are also the ones which make them hard to organize. They are the jokers in the political pack, reluctant joiners who tend to be more interested in utopia than trade unions. Unlike Oscar Wilde's philistine, they know the value of everything and the price of nothing. You would not put Arthur Rimbaud on the sanitation committee. In the 1960s and 70s, this made cultural thinkers ideal candidates for being inside and outside Marxism simultaneously. In Britain, a prominent cultural theorist like Stuart Hall occupied this position for decades, before shifting decisively into the non-Marxist camp.

To be inside and outside a position at the same time – to occupy a territory while loitering sceptically on the boundary – is often where the most intensely creative ideas stem from. It is a resourceful place to be, if not always a painless one. One has only to think of the great names of twentieth-century English literature, almost all of whom moved between two or more national cultures. Later, this ambiguity of position was to be inherited by the new 'French' cultural theorists. Not many of them were French in origin, and not many of those who were were heterosexual. Some hailed from Algeria, some from Bulgaria, and others from utopia. As the 1970s wore on, however, quite a few of these erstwhile radicals began to come in from the cold. The passage towards the depoliticized 80s and 90s had been opened.

3

The Path to Postmodernism

As the countercultural 1960s and 70s turned into the postmodern 80s and 90s, the sheer irrelevance of Marxism seemed all the more striking. For now industrial production really did seem on the way out, and along with it the proletariat. The post-war boom faded in the face of intensified international competition which forced down rates of profit. National capitalisms were now struggling to stay on their feet in an increasingly global world. They were less protected than before. As a result of this slackening in profits, the whole capitalist system was forced to undergo a dramatic make-over. Production was exported to low-wage spots in what the West fondly likes to think of as the developing world. The labour movement was bound hand and foot, forced to accept humiliating restraints on its liberties. Investment shifted away from industrial manufacture to the service, finance and communications sectors. As big business became cultural, ever more reliant on image, packaging and display, the culture industry became big business.

Yet from Marxism's own standpoint, the irony was plain. The changes which seemed to consign it to oblivion were ones it was itself in the business of explaining. Marxism was not superfluous because the system had altered its spots; it was out of favour because the system was all the more intensively what it had been before. It was plunged into crisis; and it was Marxism above all which had given an account of how such crises came and went. From Marxism's own viewpoint, then, what made it look redundant was exactly what confirmed its relevance. It had not been shown the door because the system had reformed itself, leaving socialist criticism superfluous. It had been turfed out for exactly the opposite reason. It was because the system looked too hard to beat, not because it had changed its spots, which caused many to despair of radical change.

The enduring relevance of Marxism was most evident on a global scale. It was not so obvious to those Eurocentric critics of the theory who could only see that the Yorkshire coal-mines were closing and the Western working class shrinking. On a planetary scale, the inequalities between rich and poor have continued to widen, as *The Communist Manifesto* had foreseen. As it also predicted, there is growing militant disaffection on the part of the world's poor. It is just that whereas Marx had looked for such disaffection to Bradford and the Bronx, it is to be found today in the souks of Tripoli and Damascus. And it is smallpox, not storming the Winter Palace, that some of them have in mind.

As for the disappearance of the proletariat, we should recall to mind the etymology of the word. The proletariat in ancient society were those who were too poor to serve the state by holding property, and who served it instead by producing children (*proles*, offspring) as labour power. They are those who have nothing to give but their bodies. Proletarians and women are thus intimately allied, as indeed they are in the impoverished regions of the world today. The ultimate poverty or loss of being is to be left with nothing but yourself. It is to work directly with your body, like the other animals. And since this is still the condition of millions of men and women on the planet today, it is strange to be told that the proletariat has disappeared.

In the heyday of cultural theory, then, the forces which would help to undo the left were already at their deconstructive work within it. What looked like its moment of insurgency was already the dawn of a political downturn. Ronald Reagan and Margaret Thatcher were already looming ominously over the horizon. In a decade or so's time, nobody would actually have disproved Marxism, just as no spacecraft had ever travelled beyond the edges of the universe to establish that God was not lurking there. But almost everyone now began to behave as though Marxism was not there, whatever they thought about the status of the Almighty.

Indeed, with the fall of the Soviet Union and its satellites, Marxism had quite literally disappeared from a whole sector of the globe. It was not so much answered as out of the question. You no more needed to have an opinion on it than you did on crop circles or poltergeists. In the brittle, avaricious Western world of the 1980s, it was less false than irrelevant. It was a solution to a set of questions which were no longer even on the agenda. Like the Loch Ness monster, it would make no difference even if it were true. You could continue to cultivate it on the side, as a harmless quirk or endearingly eccentric hobby, but it was not really the kind of thing to air in public unless you had a peculiarly thick skin or a pronounced masochistic streak. The earlier generation of thinkers had been post-Marxist in the sense of both distancing and drawing upon it; the new generation was post-Marxist in the sense that David Bowie is post-Darwinist.

This was a curious situation. For you did not have to be a Marxist to recognize that Marxism was not just a hypothesis which, like the extraterrestrial origins of crop circles, you could believe or disbelieve at will. It was not in the first place a hypothesis at all. Marxism – or, to put it within a wider context, socialism – had been a political movement involving millions of men and women across both countries and centuries. One thinker has described it as the greatest reform movement in human history. For good or ill, it has transformed the face of the earth. It is not just a cluster of intriguing ideas, like neo-Hegelianism or logical positivism. Nobody ever fought and died for logical positivism, though it may have sparked the odd inebriated scuffle in senior common rooms. If neo-Hegelians may occasionally have been propped against the wall and shot, it was not for being neo-Hegelians. In the so-called Third World, socialism had found a welcome among the wretched of the earth, who were not quite so eager to clasp semiotics or reception theory to their bosom. Now, however, it looked as though what had started life as an underground movement among dockers and factory workers had turned into a mildly interesting way of analysing *Wuthering Heights*.

The period when cultural theory was riding high displayed one peculiar feature. It seemed to mix politics and culture in equal measure. If there was civil rights and the peace movement, there was also sexual experiment, heightenings of consciousness and flamboyant changes of lifestyle. In this, the 1960s resembled nothing quite so much as the nineteenth-century *fin de siècle*. The closing decades of the nineteenth century were an astonishing blend of political and cultural radicalism. It is the period of both anarchism and aestheticism, *The Yellow Book* and the Second International, decadence and the great dock strike. Oscar Wilde believed in both socialism and art for art's sake. William Morris was a Marxist revolutionary who championed medieval art. In Ireland, Maud Gonne and Constance Markievicz moved easily between theatre, the women's movement, prison reform, Irish Republicanism and the Parisian avant-garde. W. B. Yeats was poet, mystic, political organizer, folklorist, occultist, theatre director and cultural commissar. In this extraordinary period, the same figures can be seen dabbling in Theosophy and demonstrating against unemployment. There were underground movements of socialist homosexuals. You could be enthralled by symbolism and syndicalism at the same time. Dope and diabolism were quite as plentiful as feminism.

Something of this heady brew was inherited by the 1960s. Both periods were marked by utopianism, sexual politics, spiritual slumming, imperial wars, gospels of peace and fellowship, pseudo-orientalism, political revolutionism, exotic art-forms, psychedelic states, returns to Nature, the unleashing of the unconscious. In fact, in some ways the 1960s was the tamer epoch – an age of love-ins and flower-power rather than of *fin-de-siècle* Satanism, more angelic than demonic. Towards the end of this period, it was the women's movement which forged the deepest links between the global and the personal, the political and the cultural. And some of this was bequeathed to later, postmodern times, which is to say to the next *fin de siècle*. Culture was a language which faced both ways, towards the personal and the political simultaneously. The same idiom could encompass anti-psychiatry and anti-colonialism.

Culture had been among other things a way of keeping radical politics warm, a continuation of it by other means. Increasingly, however, it was to become a substitute for it. In some ways, the 1980s were like the 1880s or 1960s without the politics. As leftist political hopes faded, cultural studies came to the fore. Dreams of ambitious social change were denounced as illicit 'grand narratives', more likely to lead to totalitarianism than to liberty. From Sydney to San Diego, Capetown to Tromsö, everyone was thinking small. Micropolitics broke out on a global scale. A new epic fable of the end of epic fables unfurled across the globe. From one end of a diseased planet to the other, there were calls to abandon planetary thinking. Whatever linked us –

whatever was the *same* – was noxious. Difference was the new catch-cry, in a world increasingly subject to the same indignities of starvation and disease, cloned cities, deadly weapons and CNN television.

It was ironic that postmodern thought should make such a fetish of difference, given that its own impulse was to erase the distinctions between image and reality, truth and fiction, history and fable, ethics and aesthetics, culture and economics, high and popular art, political left and right. Even so, while the brokers and financiers were drawing Huddersfield and Hong Kong ever closer, the cultural theorists were struggling to wedge them apart. Meanwhile, the End of History was complacently promulgated from a United States which looks increasingly in danger of ending it for real. There would be no more important world conflicts. It would become clear later that Islamic fundamentalists had not been paying sufficient attention when this announcement was broadcast.

'Cultural politics' had been born. But the phrase is deeply ambiguous. There had long been a recognition in radical circles that political change had to be 'cultural' to be effective. Any political change which does not embed itself in people's feelings and perceptions – which does not secure their consent, engage their desires and weave its way into their sense of identity – is unlikely to endure very long. This, roughly speaking, is what the Italian Marxist Antonio Gramsci meant by 'hegemony'. Socialist artists from the Bolsheviks to Bertolt Brecht spoke in briskly macho terms of dismantling the middle-class citizen and constructing the New Man in its place. A whole new kind of human being was needed for the new political order, with altered sense organs and bodily habits, a different kind of memory and set of drives. And it was the task of culture to provide it.

Mao's grotesque cultural revolution had learned this lesson

badly, cynically using 'culture' as a weapon in an internal power-struggle. Some anti-colonial leaders, however, had learned the lesson well: colonialist culture had to be ditched along with colonialist rule. There was no point in simply replacing wigged and robed white judges with wigged and robed black ones. But they did not imagine that culture could be a substitute for social transformation. Irish nationalists were not just fighting for green mail boxes rather than red ones. Black South Africans were not just fighting for the right to be black South Africans. There was a great deal more at stake than so-called identity politics.

There were movements like feminism, for which culture in the broad sense of the word is not an optional extra. On the contrary, it is central to feminism's political demands, the grammar in which they are framed. Value, speech, image, experience and identity are here the very language of political struggle, as they are in all ethnic or sexual politics. Ways of feeling and forms of representation are in the long run quite as crucial as childcare provision or equal pay. They are a vital part of the project of political emancipation. This had not been quite so true of traditional class politics. Mill workers in Victorian England might rise at dawn to study Shakespeare together before work, or keep precious transcripts of their working lives and local culture. But cultural activity of this kind was not integral to the struggle for better pay and conditions, in the sense that a struggle over sexist imagery is integral to feminism.

There were also, however, forms of cultural politics which divorced questions of experience and identity from their political contexts. The point was not to change the political world, but to secure one's cultural niche within it. At times, cultural politics seemed to be what you were left with when you had no other kind of politics. In Northern Ireland, for example, a conflict between Catholics and Protestants, in which the latter had enjoyed a

gerrymandered majority for decades, was gentrified as a question
of respectful relations betwen two 'cultural traditions'. Unionists
who only a few years previously had been shouting 'Kick the
Pope!' and 'Burn the Taigs!'[1] were suddenly defending British
power in Ireland in terms of margins, vibrant minorities, cultural
pluralism. In the United States, ethnicity sometimes just meant
minorities within the United States itself, rather than the millions
throughout the world doomed to a wretched existence by the
system the USA spearheaded. It meant domestic culture rather
than international politics. Abroad was still something of an
esoteric concept for the USA, despite the fact that it had devoted
considerable energy over the years to subduing various annoying
bits of it.

'Culture' is a slippery term, which can be either trivial or
momentous. A glossy colour supplement is culture, and so are
the images of emaciated Africans it offers to our eye. In Belfast
or the Basque country, culture can mean what you are prepared
to kill for. Or – for the slightly less zealous – die for. It can also
be a squabble over the merits of U2. You can be burnt to death
because of culture, or it can be a question of whether to wear that
rather fetching Pre-Raphaelite-style shirt. Like sex, culture is the
kind of phenomenon which it seems one can avoid underrating
only by overrating. In one sense it is what we live by, the act
of sense-making itself, the very social air we breathe; in another
sense it is far from what most profoundly shapes our lives.

There are, however, plenty of excuses for overrating the importance of culture in our time. If culture began to be more crucial to
capitalism in the 1960s, it had become well-nigh indistinguishable
from it by the 1990s. This, indeed, is part of what we mean by
postmodernism. In a world of film-actor Presidents, erotically

1. 'Taig' is a derogatory term for Gaelic-Irish Catholics.

alluring commodities, political spectaculars and a multi-billion-dollar culture industry, culture, economic production, political dominance and ideological propaganda seemed to have merged into a single featureless whole. Culture had always been about signs and representations; but now we had a whole society which performed permanently before the looking-glass, weaving everything it did into one vast mega-text, fashioning at every moment a ghostly mirror-image of its world which doubled it at every point. It was known as computerization.

At the same time, culture in the sense of identity had grown even more pressing. The more the system unfolded a drearily uniform culture across the planet, the more men and women aggressively championed the culture of their nation, region, neighbourhood or religion. At its bleakest, this meant that the narrower culture grew at one level, the more it was spread thin at another. Blandness found its response in bigotry. Rootless advertising executives jet-setted in the skies over those for whom not sharing the same piece of sky as themselves meant to be hardly human.

Capitalism has always pitched diverse forms of life promiscuously together – a fact which should give pause to those unwary postmodernists for whom diversity, astonishingly, is somehow a virtue in itself. Those for whom 'dynamic' is always a positive term might also care to reconsider their opinion, in the light of the most dynamically destructive system of production which humanity has ever seen. But we are now witnessing a brutally quickened version of this melt-down, with the tearing up of traditional communities, the breaking down of national barriers, the generating of great tidal waves of migration. Culture in the form of fundamentalism has reared its head in reaction to these shattering upheavals. Everywhere you look, people are prepared to go to extraordinary lengths to be themselves.

This is partly because other people have abandoned the notion of being themselves as an undue restriction on their activities.

Fundamentalism is formidably hard to budge – which should warn us against assuming that culture is endlessly malleable while Nature is always fixed. This is another dogma of postmodernists, who are perpetually on the watch for those who 'naturalize' social or cultural facts, and so make what is changeable appear permanent and inevitable. They seem not to have noticed that this view of Nature as unchangeable has itself changed rather a lot since the days of Wordsworth. Living as they apparently do in a pre-Darwinist, pre-technological world, they fail to see that Nature is in some ways much more pliable stuff than culture. It has proved a lot easier to level mountains than to change patriarchal values. Cloning sheep is child's play compared to persuading chauvinists out of their prejudices. Cultural beliefs, not least the fundamentalist variety which are bound up with fears for one's identity, are far harder to uproot than forests.

What started out in the 1960s and 70s as a critique of Marxism had ended up in the 80s and 90s as a rejection of the very idea of global politics. As the transnational corporations spread from one end of the earth to the other, the intellectuals loudly insisted that universality was an illusion. Michel Foucault thought that Marxist concepts of power were limited and that conflict was actually everywhere; the postmodern philosopher Jean Baudrillard, by contrast, doubted that the Gulf War even took place. Meanwhile, the former socialist militant Jean-François Lyotard continued his inquiries into intergalactic travel, cosmic entropy and the mass exodus of the human race from the earth after the extinction of the sun in four billion years' time. For a philosopher with a distaste for grand narratives, this seemed a remarkably broad perspective. Such had been the gradual darkening of the dissident mind. In some quarters, radical combat had given way to radical chic. On every side, erstwhile radical thinkers were trimming their sails, shaving their sideburns and drawing in their horns.

The militant politicos of the 60s had been largely optimistic: if you desired intensely enough, you could achieve what you wanted. Utopia lay just beneath the cobblestones of Paris. Cultural thinkers like Barthes, Lacan, Foucault and Derrida still felt the backwash of this utopian impulse; it was just that they no longer believed that it could be realized in practice. It was fatally compromised by the emptiness of desire, the impossibility of truth, the fragility of the subject, the lie of progress, the pervasiveness of power. As Perry Anderson writes with an agreeable flourish: these thinkers 'strafed meaning, over-ran truth, outflanked ethics and politics, and wiped out history'.[2] After the débâcle of the late 1960s, the only feasible politics seemed to lie in piecemeal resistance to a system which was here to stay. The system could be disrupted but not dismantled.

Meanwhile, you could find a kind of substitute utopia in erotic intensities, the suave pleasures of art, the delectable sensuousness of signs. All of these things promised a more general happiness. The only problem was that it would never actually arrive. The mood was what might paradoxically be called one of libertarian pessimism. The yearning for utopia was not to be given up on, but nothing was more fatal to its well-being than trying to realize it. The *status quo* was to be implacably resisted, but not in the name of alternative values – a logically impossible manoeuvre. This disenchantment, in turn, was to yield to the full-blown pessimism of some later postmodern thought. In a few years' time, the very suggestion that there had ever been the

2. Perry Anderson, *In the Tracks of Historical Materialism*, London, 1983, p. 91.

faintest glimmer of progress in human history would be greeted with withering scorn by those regularly availing themselves of anaesthetics and water closets.

Traditionally, it had been the political left which thought in universal terms, and the conservative right which preferred to be modestly piecemeal. Now, these roles have been reversed with a vengeance. At the very time when a triumphalist right has been boldly reimagining the shape of the earth, the cultural left has retreated by and large into a dispirited pragmatism. Not long after some cultural thinkers proclaimed that the grand narratives of history had finally run out of steam, a peculiarly ugly such narrative was launched in the war between capital and the Koran – or a travesty of that text. It was now the intention of the West's enemies to exterminate it rather than expropriate it. Some Western leaders, not least those with offices rather high off the ground, could be forgiven for looking back on the age of socialism with a furtive twinge of nostalgia. If only they had not battered it so full-bloodedly at the time, it might have eradicated some of the very injustices which breed suicide bombers.

Of course, this retreat of the cultural left was not chiefly its own fault. It was exactly because the political right was so ambitious that the left had grown so timorous. It had had the ground – including its own internationalist ground – cut from beneath it, leaving it with only a few precarious clumps and tufts of ideas to stand on. This, however, became a less plausible defence of the cultural left once the anti-capitalist movement came along. What that remarkable campaign demonstrated, for all its confusions and ambiguities, was that thinking globally was not the same thing as being totalitarian. One could combine local action with planetary perspectives. Whereas many on the cultural left had long given up even mentioning capitalism, let alone trying to figure out what might be put in its place. Speaking of gender or ethnicity was fine; speaking of capitalism was 'totalizing' or 'economistic'. This was especially the line of those US theorists who lived in the belly of the beast, and so had some difficulty in actually seeing it straight. It did not help that they had few recent socialist memories to draw upon.

In one sense, the shift from the 1960s to the 1990s brought theory closer to the bone. The heady abstractions of structuralism, hermeneutics and the like had given way to the more palpable realities of postmodernism and post-colonialism. Post-structuralism was a current of ideas, but postmodernism and post-colonialism were real-life formations. There was a difference, at least for those tiresome theoretical dinosaurs who believed that there was more to the world than discourse, between studying the floating signifier on the one hand, and investigating Hindu nationalism or the culture of the shopping mall on the other. Yet while this return to the concrete was a homecoming to be welcomed, it was, like almost all human phenomena, not entirely positive. For one thing, it was typical of a society which believed only in what it could touch, taste and sell. For another thing, many of the more *recherché* ideas of earlier days were only apparently remote from social and political life. Hermeneutics, as the art of deciphering language, taught us to be suspicious of the glaringly self-evident. Structuralism gave us insight into the hidden codes and conventions which governed social behaviour, thus making that behaviour appear less natural and spontaneous. Phenomenology integrated high theory with everyday experience. Reception theory examined the role of the reader in literature, but was really part of a wider political concern with popular participation. The passive consumer of literature had to make way for the active co-creator. The secret was finally out that readers were quite as vital to the existence of writing as authors, and this downtrodden, long-despised class of men and women were finally girding their political loins. If 'All power to the soviets!' had something of a musty ring to it, it could at least be rewritten as 'All power to the readers!'

What has recently grown up, especially in the United States, is a kind of anti-theory. At the very moment when the United States government is flexing its muscles more insolently than ever, some cultural theory has begun to find the very word 'theory' objectionable. This had always been the case with some so-called radical feminists, who distrusted theory as an imperious assertion of the male intellect. Theory was just a lot of callow, emotionally arrested men comparing the length of their polysyllables. Anti-theory, however, means more than wanting nothing to do with theory. In that case, Brad Pitt and Barbra Streisand would qualify as anti-theorists. It means the kind of scepticism of theory which is theoretically interesting. The anti-theorist is like a doctor who gives you sophisticated medical reasons for eating as much junk food as you can swallow, or a theologian who provides you with unbeatable arguments for committing adultery.

For anti-theorists like Richard Rorty and Stanley Fish, theory is how you try to justify your way of life.[3] It gives you some fundamental reasons for what you do. But this, for anti-theorists, is neither possible nor necessary. You cannot justify your way of life by theory because theory is part of that way of life, not something set apart from it. What counts as a legitimate reason or a valid idea will be determined for you by your way of life itself. So cultures have no foundation in reason. They just do what they do. You can justify this or that bit of your behaviour, but you cannot give reasons for your way of life or

3. See, for example, Richard Rorty, *Contingency, Irony, and Solidarity*, Cambridge, 1989, and Stanley Fish, *Doing What Comes Naturally*, Oxford, 1989.

set of beliefs as a whole. It would be like saying that Peru is a bad thing.

This is the latest form of what the middle ages knew as the heresy of fideism. Your life is based on certain beliefs which are immune to rational scrutiny. Faith moves in a different sphere from reason. You did not choose your beliefs on any rational grounds; instead, like chicken-pox, they chose you. They are now so much part of you that you could not even get a fix on them if you tried. Culture is just not the kind of thing that could be or needs to be justified, any more than you need to back up why you have just clipped your toe-nails with a string of intricately metaphysical explanations, each one more baroque than the other. And this also means that there are no rational grounds for judging between cultures. I cannot judge between my culture and yours, because my judgement is bound to be made from *within* my own culture, not from some disinterested point outside it. There is no such place to stand. So either we are inside or complicit, or outside and irrelevant.

It is gratifying that we do not need to back what we do with theoretical explanations, because this would be impossible anyway. Since our culture is what we are made out of, it would mean that we would have to leap out of our skins, see ourselves seeing something, reflect on the very forces which make us human subjects in the first place. We would have to scrutinize ourselves as though we were not there. But it is impossible to haul ourselves up by our cultural bootstraps in this way. We could never launch a total, full-blooded critique of our way of life, because we would not be around to do it. Anyway, since we only work as human beings within the terms of our particular culture, such a total criticism would be unintelligible to us. It would have to spring from somewhere utterly beyond the categories of our experience, as though from some unusually literate zebra who had been assiduously taking notes on our cultural habits. A fundamental criticism of what we are would be bound to pass us by. It simply could not intersect with our everyday language.

This whole case is alarming in one sense and consoling in another. It is alarming because it suggests that our culture has no solid basis. The fact that we value Pushkin or free speech is purely contingent. We just happened to be born into the sort of set-up which admires those kinds of thing. It could easily have been otherwise, and elsewhere in the world it *is* otherwise. Whether grief, compassion, right-angled triangles or the concept of something being the case are equally culturally contingent is perhaps harder to establish. When we get down to such things as not toasting each other's health in sulphuric acid, the picture begins to blur a little. There are a lot of things that we do because we are the kind of animals we are, not because we are nuns or Macedonians. The idea, anyway, is that nothing needs to be the way it is, and that therefore the way things are does not need to be justified at the deepest level.

If this thought is consoling, it is partly because it saves us having to engage in a lot of strenuous mental labour, and partly because there are rather a lot of things in our culture which would be pretty hard to justify. It is not clear whether on this viewpoint torture is just something we happen to do, rather like playing tennis. Even if it is something we shouldn't do, as the anti-theorists would surely agree, the reasons why we shouldn't do it are themselves contingent ones. They have nothing to do with the way human beings are, since human beings are no way in particular. We just happen to belong to a culture which disapproves of forcing confessions out of people by holding their heads down in water for long periods of time. And of course we think our culture is right to hold this view – but that is also because we belong to it.

Not many thinkers are bold-faced enough to go entirely relativist on such issues and claim that if torture happens to be in
your tradition, then more power to your elbow. Most of them
would claim, with varying degrees of reluctance and liberal guilt,
that torture is wrong for such people, too. Most people, if they
had to choose, would rather be seen as cultural imperialists
than champions of cruelty. It is just that for the anti-theorists,
reality itself has no views about whether torture is admirable or
repulsive. In fact, reality has no views about anything. Moral
values, like everything else, are a matter of random, free-floating
cultural traditions.

There is no need to be alarmed about this, however, since
human culture is not *really* free-floating. Which is not to say
that it is firmly anchored either. That would be just the flipside
of the same misleading metaphor. Only something which was
capable of being anchored could be described as having floated
loose. We would not call a cup 'floating loose' just because it
wasn't clamped to the table with bands of steel. Culture only
seems free-floating because we once thought we were riveted in
something solid, like God or Nature or Reason. But that was
an illusion. It is not that it was once true but now is not, but
that it was false all along. We are like someone crossing a high
bridge and suddenly being seized by panic on realizing that there
is a thousand-foot drop below them. It is as though the ground
beneath their feet is no longer solid. But in fact it is.

This is one difference between modernism and postmodernism.
Modernism, or so it imagined, was old enough to remember a
time when there were firm foundations to human existence, and
was still reeling from the shock of their being kicked rudely
away. This is one reason why so much modernism is of a tragic
temper. The drama of Samuel Beckett, for example, has no faith
whatsoever in redemption, but presents a world which still looks

as though it is in dire need of it. It refuses to turn its gaze from the intolerableness of things, even if there is no transcendent consolation at hand. After a while, however, you can ease the strain of this by portraying a world in which there is indeed no salvation, but on the other hand nothing to be saved. This is the post-tragic realm of postmodernism. Postmodernism is too young to remember a time when there was (so it was rumoured) truth, identity and reality, and so feels no dizzying abyss beneath its feet. It is used to treading clear air, and has no sense of giddiness. In a reverse of the phantom limb syndrome, there seems to be something missing but there is not. We are simply the prisoners of a deceptive metaphor here, imagining as we do that the world has to stand on something in the way that we stand on the world. It is not that the pure ice beneath our feet has yielded to rough ground; the ground was rough all along.

We are like toddlers who still insist that they need their comforters, and need to be dragged kicking and screaming to the recognition that they do not. To relinquish our metaphysical comforters would be to make the momentous discovery that doing so has changed absolutely nothing. If only we could accept this we would be thoroughly post-metaphysical, and hence free. As Nietzsche admonished us, however, we have killed God but hidden the body, insisting as we do on behaving as though he is still alive. Postmodernism exhorts us to recognize that we will lose nothing by the crumbling of the foundations except our chains. We can now do what we want, without carting around a lot of cumbersome metaphysical baggage in order to justify it. Having checked in our baggage, we have freed our hands.

It seems, however, that anti-theorists like Fish and Rorty may simply have replaced one kind of anchoring with another. It is now culture, not God or Nature, which is the foundation of the world. It is not, to be sure, all that stable a foundation, since cultures change, and there are many varieties of them. But while we are actually inside a culture we cannot peer outside it, so that it feels like as much of a foundation as Reason did to Hegel. Indeed, what we would see if we could peer beyond it would itself be determined by the culture. Culture, then, is a bumpy kind of bottom line, but it is a bottom line all the same. It goes all the way down. Instead of doing what comes naturally, we do what comes culturally. Instead of following Nature, we follow Culture. Culture is a set of spontaneous habits so deep that we can't even examine them. And this, among other things, conveniently insulates them from criticism.

We can, perhaps, be ironic about our deepest commitments, acknowledging their arbitrariness, but this does not really slacken their grip upon us. Irony does not go as far down as belief. Culture thus becomes the new Nature, which can no more be called into question than a waterfall. Naturalizing things gives way to culturalizing them. Either way, they come to appear inevitable. Since everyone in a hard-nosed, streetwise age has now seen through the strategy of 'naturalizing', you need a different, more fashionable way of lending your way of life legitimacy. And this is the concept of culture. If cultures are contingent, they can always be changed; but they cannot be changed as a whole, and the reasons we have for changing them are also contingent.

What are we to make of this argument? It may well be that cultural habits like imagining time as flowing forward, or perceiving other human bodies as persons, run so deep in us that we could not possibly think ourselves outside them. But the same can scarcely be said for cultural habits like banning customers who are not wearing evening dress from hot-dog stalls, or refusing to forgive the debt of impoverished nations. The trick of some anti-theorists is to make these two kinds of case appear the same. And this makes it seem that we could no more get out of NATO than we could get out of our bodies. Another anti-theoretical stratagem is to claim that in order to launch some fundamental critique of our culture, we would need to be standing at some impossible Archimedean point beyond it. What this fails to see is that reflecting critically on our situation is part of our situation. It is a feature of the peculiar way we belong to the world. It is not some impossible light-in-the-refrigerator attempt to scrutinize ourselves when we are not there. Curving back upon ourselves is as natural to us as it is to cosmic space or a wave of the sea. It does not entail jumping out of our own skin. Without such self-monitoring, we would not have survived as a species.

This, in fact, is one important way in which we do indeed diverge from our fellow animals, whatever may usefully be said about our mutual affinities. It is not that human beings interpret the world whereas other animals do not. All sensuous response to reality is an interpretation of it. Beetles and monkeys clearly interpret their world, and act on the basis of what they see. Our physical senses are themselves organs of interpretation. What distinguishes us from our fellow animals is that we are able in turn to interpret these interpretations. In that sense, all human language is meta-language. It is a second-order reflection on the 'language' of our bodies – of our sensory apparatus.

It is this which cultural theory's inflation of the role of language (an error native to intellectuals, as melancholia is endemic among clowns) has tended to play down. At its crudest, this slides towards the case that language and experience are indissociable, as though no baby ever cried because it was hungry. What the baby lacks is not the experience of hunger, but the ability to identify this experience for what it is through an act of symbolization, placing it within a wider context. And this can come to it only from culture. It is this culture which language brings with it. Even when I have language, however, my sensory experience still represents a kind of surplus over it. The body is not reducible to signification, as linguistic reductionists tend to imagine. Some of this overestimating of the role of language in human affairs may spring from the fact that philosophers were traditionally bachelor dons who had no experience of small children. English aristocrats, who on the whole prefer hounds and horses to human beings, have never bulked large in the ranks of linguistic inflationists.

One can reasonably claim that pre-linguistic infants can have beliefs and act on the basis of reasons.[4] What they cannot do is ask themselves moral questions such as whether their beliefs are sound or whether their reasons are good ones. Only a linguistic animal can be a moral one. Infants and aardvarks can desire what they think is good, but they cannot want to desire what is good. Even so, infants appear to recognize, discriminate, investigate, re-identify and classify, and all this without the aid of language. So also, it can be claimed, do non-human animals. Non-human animals behave as though they have beliefs, which is not to say that they are social democrats or orthodox Jews. Some dolphins can distinguish the sentence 'Take the surfboard to the frisbee' from 'Take the frisbee to the surfboard', an operation which even some world leaders might find difficulty with.

Self-reflection, then – interpreting our sensory interpretations – is part of what we are. And this may be conducted in full-blooded critical spirit. There is no need to struggle out of your skin in order to make fundamental criticisms of your situation. You do not have to be standing in metaphysical outer space to recognize the injustice of racial discrimination. This is exactly where you would

4. See Alasdair MacIntyre, *Dependent Rational Animals*, London, 1999, ch. 4.

not recognize it. On the contrary, there is a good deal *within* our culture which we can draw on to do so. Anti-theorists make the mistake of seeing cultures as more or less coherent. So criticism of them comes either from the outside, in which case it is irrelevant or unintelligible, or from the inside, in which case it is not really radical. But there are many different, contradictory strands to a culture, some of which allow us to be critical of others. To act according to the Western way of life may mean to throw up barricades in Piccadilly just as much as to tear them down. If scones and cream represent one English cultural tradition, the suffragettes represent another. It is good news that we cannot entirely escape our culture – for if we could, we would not be able to submit it to critical judgement.

In a similar way, comparing two cultures does not mean having no cultural vantage-point of your own. The fact that cultures can look beyond themselves is part of what they are. It is a fact about cultures that their boundaries are porous and ambiguous, more like horizons than electrified fences. Our cultural identity leaks beyond itself just by virtue of what it is, not as an agreeable bonus or disagreeable haemorrhage. There may, of course, be serious difficulties in translating from one culture to another. But you do not need to be standing at some imaginary Omega point in order to do this, any more than you need to resort to some third language in order to translate from Swedish into Swahili. Being inside a culture is not like being inside a prison-house. It is more like being inside a language. Languages open on to the world from the inside. To be inside a language is to be pitched into the world, not to be quarantined from it.

The point for the anti-theorists, then, is just to get on with what we do, without all this distracting fuss about theory. We should forget about 'deep' legitimations: depth is just what we put there ourselves, and then find ourselves predictably awestruck by. It is true that we can no longer justify our practices in some full-blooded metaphysical way; but this does not leave them vulnerable, since neither can those who take us to task. So as far as such deep talk goes, we might as well call a truce. Philosophy becomes anti-philosophy. For some modern thinkers, thinking about what you are doing will seriously disable it, just as it is inadvisable to think about the physiology of your thighs during a hurdle race. Reflecting on what you are doing may well prove dangerous for hurdlers, but it seems a strange conclusion for those who are highly paid for thinking.

For Nietzsche and Freud, however, we can operate as human beings only by repressing much of what goes into our making. It is our nature to be anti-theoretical, even if we need theory to uncover the fact. Too much repression, to be sure, will make us fall ill; but for this deeply anti-Romantic view, repression is not an evil in itself. We could not speak, think or act without it. Only by self-oblivion can we be ourselves. Amnesia, not remembrance, is what is natural to us. The ego is what it is only by a necessary blindness to much of what constitutes it. To make history, we need first to blot out the squalid, blood-stained genealogy which went into our manufacture. In another sense, this idea is Romantic enough: the intellect is the death of spontaneity. Reflecting too sensitively on the world around you paralyses action, as Hamlet discovered. Or, to translate the sentiment into part of what lurks behind the anti-theory case: If we raise questions about the foundations of our way of life, in the sense of thinking too much about the barbarism on which our civilization is founded, we might fail to do the things that all good citizens should spontaneously do.

The period from 1965 to 1980 was by no means the first outbreak of revolutionary cultural ideas in twentieth-century Europe. For all its excitement, it pales to a shadow before the great current of modernism which swept the continent earlier in the century. If one wanted to select another, more distinguished decade-and-a-half which transformed European culture, one could do worse than choose 1910 to 1925. In this brief span of years, that culture was shattered and remade. It was the age of Proust, Joyce, Pound, Kafka, Rilke, Mann, Eliot, Futurism, Surrealism and a good deal more. As with the 1960s, it was also a time of tumultuous social change – though nothing in the later period compares in scale to the wars, revolutions and social upheavals of the earlier. If the 1960s and 70s witnessed bouts of left-wing insurgency, the earlier period saw the birth of the first workers' state in history. If the 1960s and 70s were an age of colonial revolutions, the years from 1910 to 1925 had at their centre the greatest imperialist conflagration which history had ever witnessed.

Modernism reflected the crack-up of a whole civilization. All the beliefs which had served nineteenth-century middle-class society so splendidly – liberalism, democracy, individualism, scientific inquiry, historical progress, the sovereignty of reason – were now in crisis. There was a dramatic speed-up in technology, along with widespread political instability. It was becoming hard to believe that there was any innate order in the world. Instead, what order we discovered in the world was one we had put there ourselves. Realism in art, which had taken such an order for granted, began to buckle and implode. A cultural form which had been riding high since the Renaissance now seemed to be approaching exhaustion.

In all these ways, modernism anticipated the later outbreak of cultural theory. In fact, cultural theory was among other things the continuation of modernism by other means. By about 1960, the great works of modernism had begun to lose much of their disturbing force. Joyce and Kafka were welcomed on to the university syllabuses, while modernist works of painting proved to be lucrative commodities with which no self-respecting corporation could dispense. The middle classes flocked to the concert halls to be archly scandalized by Schoenberg, while the stark, wasted figures of Beckett stalked the London stage. Brecht was de-alienated and a whole raft of fascist fellow-travellers politically sanitized. The outrageously experimental T. S. Eliot was awarded the prestigious Order of Merit. The dissident impulse behind the modernist movement still survived here and there, lingering on in late Surrealism and Situationism. But the movement as a whole had run out of subversive steam.

That dissident impulse needed to migrate elsewhere; and cultural theory was one place where it set up home. Writers like Barthes, Foucault, Kristeva and Derrida were really late modernist artists who had taken to philosophy rather than to sculpture or the novel. They had a touch of the flair and iconoclastic force of the great modernist artists, as well as inheriting their intimidatory aura. The boundaries between the conceptual and the creative began to blur. This was one reason why less imaginatively endowed philosophers did not only denounce these thinkers; they failed to recognize what they were doing as philosophy at all. This was curious, since philosophy – to give the subject as rigorous a definition as possible – means speaking about certain things in certain ways. Time is a legitimate topic of philosophy, but Proust does not talk about it in the right way. Death is not in everyone's view a valid philosophical concept, but if you discussed it in the language of Donald Davidson rather than Martin Heidegger, it might become so. Personal identity happens to be a pukka philosophical topic at present, but suffering is not quite so kosher. Besides, these French thinkers were clearly on the political left, whereas orthodox philosophers were not political at all. They were, in other words, conservative.

Why, then, had cultural theory ousted cultural practice? One answer is simply because that cultural practice, in the shape of high-modernist art, already existed. Nothing ever happens twice, precisely because it has happened once already. The major art of twentieth-century Europe was the fruit of the first, traumatic impact on cultural life of the crisis of modern Western civilization. Once that impact had occurred, it was hard to feel it again in all its shocking immediacy. It is not easy to have the ground cut a second time from beneath one's feet, unless one lives on the San Andreas fault. We became used to living with the loss of absolute value, along with the belief that progress was a myth, human reason an illusion and our existence a futile passion. We had grown accustomed to our *angst*, and had begun to hug our lack of chains.

In any case, the full scandalousness of these ideas shows up only against the background of a traditional, relatively stable culture. That was a background which was still perceptible in 1920, but fading rapidly by 1970. By the time postmodernism heaved over the horizon, there was little memory of such a context at all. As the pace of capitalist enterprise quickened, instability, disruption, perversity and sensationalism were now the order of the day. They were not particularly offensive, since there was no norm to measure them against. It was not as though they could be contrasted with the values of the family hearth. The hearth was the place where the family soaked up perversity, disruption and sensationalism on television.

Modernism, like the culture of the 1960s and 70s, could take it for granted that when it came to the cultural establishment, realism was still dominant. Indeed, it has proved perhaps the most resilient cultural form in Western history, beating off all contenders. And this suggests that it has at least some of its roots deep in the Western psyche. What was valuable was the kind of art which mirrored a world in which you could recognize yourself. Quite *why* this is thought valuable is extremely hard to say. The answer probably has more to do with magic than aesthetics. It is not easy to say why we take such an infantile pleasure in gazing at an image of a banana which looks for all the world like a banana.

Realism, then, was what the new movements were out to disrupt. But their experiments in art and thought were to that extent still dependent on it. We would not find a Cubist painting arresting unless we were accustomed to non-Cubist canvases. Dissonance is reliant on a sense of harmony. In some ways, the modernist assault on realism had failed. By the 1930s, realism was firmly back in the saddle. In the 1960s and 70s, the new cultural theory made another valiant effort to dislodge it, summoning modernist art to its aid. This incursion, too, however, was largely routed. Yet what nobody could have predicted was that Western civilization was just on the brink of going non-realist itself. Reality itself had now embraced the non-realist, as capitalist society became increasingly dependent in its everyday operations on myth and fantasy, fictional wealth, exoticism and hyperbole, rhetoric, virtual reality and sheer appearance.

This, then, was one of the roots of postmodernism. Postmodernism gets off the ground when it is no longer a matter of having information about the world, but a matter of the world as information. Suddenly, anti-realism was no longer just a question of theory. How could you conceivably represent in realist terms the great invisible criss-crossing circuits of communication, the incessant buzzing to and fro of signs, which was contemporary society? How could you represent Star Wars, or the prospect of millions dead in a biological attack? Perhaps the end of representation would come when there was nobody left to represent, or to be represented. The radical modernists had tried to dismantle the distinction between art and life. Now, it seemed that life had done it for them. But whereas the radical modernists had in mind such things as reading your poetry through megaphones in factory yards, postmodernism had in mind for the most part such things as advertising and public relations. A left-wing subcurrent of it tried to reinvent more dissident ways of integrating culture into social life, but could scarcely compete with the manufacture of political spectaculars or reality TV shows. A radical assault on fixed hierarchies of value merged effortlessly with that revolutionary levelling of all values known as the marketplace.

The emotional climates of modernism and the 1960s were very diffferent. Both were wreathed in the euphoria and effervescence one associates with a sudden outbreak of modernization. Modernism as a cultural movement is among other things a response to the alarming, exhilarating impact of large-scale modernization on previously traditional societies. This is one reason why the only major home-grown (as opposed to imported) modernism in the United Kingdom was in culturally traditionalist, politically turbulent, newly modernizing Ireland. Even if a good deal of modernism is fiercely critical of those innovatory forces, it still catches up something of their buoyancy and exuberance. In general, however, the tone of the modernist period was anxious and agonized, whereas the tone of the 1960s was cool and casual. Modernism was haunted by apocalyptic visions of the collapse of civilization, whereas the 1960s tended to greet the prospect with acclaim. Only some of its dreams of apocalypse were drug-induced.

Modernism and cultural theory were both international movements. Both were disdainful of parochialism, of either mental or physical space. The typical modernist artists were exiles and émigrés, and so were some of the foremost cultural thinkers of the later age. Like the revolutionary working class, the modernist artists acknowledged no homeland, crossing national frontiers as easily as they glided from one art-form or coterie or manifesto to another. Huddled together in some polyglot metropolis, they set up home in art rather than in nation-states. In that way, they could compensate among other things for the loss of a genuine homeland and a national tradition. Modernism was a hybrid affair, mixing together fragments of various national cultures. If the traditional world was now in pieces, if every human identity was now a collage, the modernists would pluck an artistic virtue from that historical necessity, scavenging resourcefully among the rubble of clapped-out ideologies in the manner of Baudelaire's ragpickers to fashion some wondrous new creations.

In a similar way, cultural theory was later to roll across linguistics, philosophy, literature, politics, art, anthropology and so on, breaching traditional academic barriers as it went. It was a library cataloguer's nightmare. The names 'structuralism', 'theory', 'cultural studies' were merely provisional signposts, rather as 'existentialism' had been for a previous generation. As with existentialism, the new cultural ideas concerned profound changes in everyday life as well as academia, in tastes, sensibilities, social values and moral agendas. At the same time, theory burst the dam between popular and minority culture: you could try on a structuralist reading of *Popeye the Sailorman* just as readily as you could of *Paradise Lost*. Like high-modernist art, however, theory's treatment of popular culture was at first something of a *de haut en bas* affair. Whether with T. S. Eliot on music hall or Roland Barthes on wrestling, both movements stooped to the demotic without detriment to their aura. It was postmodernism which marked the break here, as both theory and art became conspicuously classless and consumer-friendly. Those left-wing theorists who had dreamed of a classless social order had only to open their eyes to see that it had already arrived and was known as the shopping mall.

Both periods, too, were times of spiritual extremism. Like language and artistic form, men and women would reveal the truth about themselves only when pressed to a limit. In demanding your rights, why not ask for everything while you were about it? Why compromise with outmoded forms, pouring new wine into old bottles? It was not just a matter of thinking new thoughts; the very frames of our thinking needed to be broken and refashioned. Neither was it just a question of producing new literature or philosophy, but of inventing a whole new way of writing. Philosophers like Martin Heidegger, Theodor Adorno and Jacques Derrida could say what they meant only by forging new literary styles, bursting the bounds between poetry and philosophy. You had to use concepts but at the same time point to their limits, highlight their boundaries, implode them from the inside; and this was a kind of equivalent of modernist irony. Politically speaking, you needed to construct a new type of human being who would not just refrain from violence and exploitation, but who would be physically and morally incapable of it. The entire world was trembling on the brink of apocalypse, and keeping faith with your impossible desire would carry you over the edge. The past was a write-off, eternity was now, and the future had just landed.

Despite the torrent of ideas to which both periods gave birth, they shared a deep suspicion of human reason. Modernism reacted to a top-heavy Victorian rationalism by turning to the exotic, the primitivist, the archaic and unconscious. Truth was to be felt in the guts and genitals, not in the head. Animal spontaneity was the latest cerebral experiment. For all its self-conscious modernity, it was a period rife with myth and sour with blood and soil. A figure like D. H. Lawrence, with his celebration of the dark gods, is exemplary here. We would be blown backwards into the future by gazing on the archaic images of the past, a past which resembled utopia in its absolute non-existence.

The 1960s also turned to cults of happy mind-blowing, along with bogus forms of the primitive and oriental. A glazed innocence stalked abroad. Intellectuals delivered erudite lectures on the value of pure mindlessness, while ageing hippies danced naked in Hyde Park. Schizophrenics were heralded as harbingers of a new form of consciousness. Men and women believed fervently in expanding the mind, but more with dope than with doses of Virgil. In both cases, it was sometimes hard to distinguish between creative challenges to reason, and plain old-fashioned irrationalism. Did you need a whole new kind of consciousness, or was consciousness itself the problem? Was logic a ruling-class conspiracy? 'We do not want to destroy kapital [*sic*] because it is not rational,' announced Jean-François Lyotard, 'but because it is.'[5] In both periods, there was a flight from the intellect to the simple rural life or the cloudy depths of the unconscious, to tropical islands, concrete poetry, raw sensations or psychedelic visions. Reflection was the problem, not the solution.

The 1960s and 70s witnessed a great deal of highly sophisticated theory; but a lot of it, ironically, was fascinated by what escaped theorizing altogether. On the whole, it valued what could not be thought more highly than what could. What was needed was a theory beyond theory. If concepts belonged to the degenerate language of the present, then whatever eluded their clammy grasp might bring us a glimpse of utopia. Desire, difference, the body, the unconscious, pleasure, the floating signifier: all these things finally baffled theory, to theory's masochistic

5. Quoted in Anderson, *The Origins of Postmodernity*, p. 27.

delight. To recognize this, however, demanded a good deal of rigorous thought. It took a subtle thinker to explore the limits of thought. Theory was a kind of homoeopathy, using reflection in order to get us beyond it. But this was different from the philistine complacency of the later anti-theorists, whose advice to theorists could be summed up in Richard Rorty's folksy admonition: 'Don't scratch where it doesn't itch.'

Finally, what modernism and 'high' cultural theory shared in common was their many-sided ambitiousness. Both were prepared to venture into perilous territory, chance their arm and broach issues of ultimate importance. New concepts were forged and new methods elaborated. The explorations of these writers ranged across politics and sexuality, language and culture, ethics and economics, the psyche and human civilization. Today's cultural theory is somewhat more modest. It dislikes the idea of depth, and is embarrassed by fundamentals. It shudders at the notion of the universal, and disapproves of ambitious overviews. By and large, it can see such overviews only as oppressive. It believes in the local, the pragmatic, the particular. And in this devotion, ironically, it scarcely differs from the conservative scholarship it detests, which likewise believes only in what it can see and handle.

There is, however, a much deeper irony. At just the point that we have begun to think small, history has begun to act big. 'Act locally, think globally' has become a familiar leftist slogan; but we live in a world where the political right acts globally and the postmodern left thinks locally. As the grand narrative of capitalist globalization, and the destructive reaction which it brings in its wake, unfurls across the planet, it catches these intellectuals at a time when many of them have almost ceased to think in political terms at all. Confronted with an implacable political enemy, and a fundamentalist one at that, the West will no doubt be forced more and more to reflect on the foundations of its own civilization.

It must do so, however, at the very time when the philosophers are arriving hot-foot with the news that there are no such foundations in the first place. The bad news is that the Emperor is naked. The West, then, may need to come up with some persuasive-sounding legitimations of its form of life, at exactly the point when laid-back cultural thinkers are assuring it that such legitimations are neither possible nor necessary. It may be forced to reflect on the truth and reality of its existence, at a time when postmodern thought has grave doubts about both truth and reality. It will need, in short, to sound deep in a progressively more shallow age.

The inescapable conclusion is that cultural theory must start thinking ambitiously once again – not so that it can hand the West its legitimation, but so that it can seek to make sense of the grand narratives in which it is now embroiled. Before we examine what this might mean, however, we need to draw up a balance sheet of cultural theory's gains and losses so far.

4

Losses and Gains

For some of its critics, the very idea of cultural theory is a contradiction in terms, rather like 'fascist intellectual' or 'Alabaman *haute cuisine*'. The whole point of art and literature is their particularity. Works of art and culture are living experiences, not abstract doctrines. They are sensuous, delicate, uniquely individual. Don't abstract ideas simply kill all this dead? Isn't a theory of art rather like trying to have a science of scowling or cuddling? You cannot have a science of the individual. Entomologists study insect life, but they would not study a single spider and nothing more. Theory is general, culture is specific. Even if we take culture in a wider sense, to mean the ways in which a group of people make symbolic sense of their situation, we are still talking about their lived experience. And it is hard to see how there can be a theory of this.

In fact, all talk about art is abstract. Cultural theory is not exceptional in this respect. You can speak of the haunting way in which the tone of the poem shifts from despondency to lyrical exultation, but to do so is to speak in abstractions. The word 'symbol' is quite as abstract as the word 'signifier'. It is just that most people have grown used to the first but not the second. A lot of so-called ordinary language is just jargon which we have forgotten is jargon. 'Character' and 'monologue' are not jargon any longer, whereas 'class struggle' and 'patriarchal' still are. 'Her gracious Majesty the Queen' is jargon, but not for a British royalist. 'Secondary carcinoma' is jargon for hair stylists but not for surgeons. Jargon often enough means ideas you happen not to agree with. A former editor of the *Times Literary Supplement* declared rather piously that he always put a blue pencil through words like 'discourse'. For his predecessors in the editorial chair, it was probably words like 'montage' and 'neurotic'. Perhaps for *their* predecessors it was 'evolution' and 'sociology'.

In any case, the assumption that all art is vividly particular is of fairly recent vintage. For all its love of the particular, this assumption oddly pretends to be a universal truth. It was only from about the late eighteenth century that art was redefined in this way. Samuel Johnson thought that the particular was tedious and the universal exciting. It is highly unlikely that Virgil, Euripides, Dante, Rabelais or Shakespeare viewed art in this light. Indeed, it is highly unlikely that they had anything like the concept of art which we have today, or in some cases a concept of art at all. The notion of art which we take for granted nowadays was invented only about two centuries ago. Nor has it passed unchallenged. A century or so after its birth, it came under heavy fire from the modernist movement.

It is true, to misquote George Orwell, that all language is abstract but some language more abstract than others. But this is not necessarily the difference between theory and other ways of talking about art and culture. Samuel Taylor Coleridge and T. S. Eliot, who are not usually seen as 'theorists', are sometimes quite as abstract as Jacques Derrida. You can write about the jagged contours of a narrative or the grainy texture of a phrase; but these are *acceptable* forms of jargon, as some other kinds of art-talk are not. Indeed, this kind of acceptable jargon is the house-style or *patois* of contemporary criticism. It is as instantly recognizable from Sydney to San Diego as a crooked finger is to a Freemason. Becoming a literary critic today means learning to be fluent in this sort of language.

If 'hermeneutical phenomenology' counts as jargon, so does the on-the-job language of dockers and motor mechanics. If pig farmers can find lawyers obscure, lawyers can find pig farmers mystifying. Sometimes it is jargon we need, and sometimes ordinary language. We do not mind if the doctor asks us how the old tummy is getting along, but if he were to write 'Old tummy playing up a bit' on his clinical notes, our confidence in his professional abilities might take a knock. If an art critic writes that there's a very nice sort of funny little red thing in the centre of the canvas, we might begin to wonder whether the public resources lavished on her education were really justified. We do not want sailors to talk about that thing you crank the life-boats down with. There are many situations in life when we would feel unhappy if we understood what was being said. 'A bit to the left, then sort of drift along for a while' is not quite what we want to hear from air traffic control over our captain's radio.

Even so, this hardly excuses a prominent literary theorist perpetrating a sentence like 'The in-choate in-fans ab-original para-subject cannot be theorized as functionally *completely* frozen in a world where teleology is schematized into geo-graphy.' In infant school, breaking up words with hyphens was a way of understanding them better; here, it is a silly affectation which has the opposite effect. This kind of jargon is as much a badge of tribal belonging as the stethoscope trailing ostentatiously from a physician's pocket. It is not just that sentences like these are incomprehensible to the toiling masses; they are incomprehensible to most of the non-toiling intelligentsia as well. Sometimes, one suspects, they might even be only dimly intelligible to those who produce them. People who write like this are not even interested in being understood. To write in this way as a *literary* academic, someone who is actually paid for having among other things a certain flair and feel for language, is rather like being a myopic optician or a grossly obese ballet dancer. Whereas rock stars and footballers need ghost writers to make them sound more intelligent and articulate, authors like this need ghost writers to make their prose more stupid and simple-minded.

Not that all theorists write as wretchedly as this. In fact, some of them – Theodor Adorno, Roland Barthes, Michel Foucault, Fredric Jameson – rank among the great literary stylists of our time. You can be difficult without being obscure. Difficulty is a matter of content, whereas obscurity is a question of how you present that content. It is true that there are some ideas, not least in science, which cannot be adequately simplified. Not all wisdom is simple and spontaneous. 'The secret of all great art is its simplicity' is simplistic nonsense. Yet it is possible to write clearly about some esoteric issues, just as some theorists manage with heroic perversity to write esoterically about plain ones.

There is something particularly scandalous about *radical* cultural theory being so wilfully obscure. Not because it could reach hordes of the labouring masses if only it used shorter words. It is scandalous because the whole idea of cultural theory is at root a democratic one. In the bad old days, it was assumed that culture was something you needed to have in your blood, like malaria or red corpuscles. Countless generations of breeding went into the way a gentleman could instantly distinguish a sprightly metaphor from a shopsoiled one. Culture was not really something you could acquire, any more than you could acquire a second pair of eyebrows or learn how to have an erection. Civility was what came naturally. Your judgements on Stendhal and Rembrandt were as spontaneous as a sneeze, as instinctive as opening doors for elderly ladies. Theory, which as we have seen was born somewhere in the dense, democratic jungle of the 1960s, thought otherwise. All you needed in order to join in the game was to learn certain ways of talking, not to have a couple of thoroughbreds tethered outside the door. And these ways of talking were in principle open to anyone.

No layperson opens a botany textbook and shuts it with an irascible bang if they do not understand it straight away. Since art and culture are at least as complex as the life of plants, it would be strange if talk about them were any more instantly comprehensible. Yet a lot of people who are not surprised to find botany hard going are mildly outraged not to be able to understand an account of a sculpture or a novel. And this is for an interesting reason. Art and culture are supposed to deal with 'human' questions rather than with 'technical' ones – with love, death and desire, rather than with the law of tort or the organic structure of decapods. And we can surely all understand the 'human'. In fact, this is a fairly dubious distinction. For Aristotle, being human was in a sense a technical affair, as was love for Thomas Aquinas, desire for Sigmund Freud, and as death is for a mortician. And it is not easy to sort out the 'human' from the 'technical' in the case of art.

Art, however, seems in principle available to anybody, in a way that knowing about the organic structure of decapods is not. In fact, some essays about decapods are probably a lot easier to read than Joyce's *Ulysses* or the poetry of Paul Celan. With modernism, the language of art begins to diverge radically from the language of everyday life, in a way that George Eliot would no doubt have found surprising. People may sometimes have spoken rather like *Adam Bede*, but nobody ever spoke like *Finnegans Wake*. With postmodernism, however, the two idioms are drawn closer together: the language of the media and a good deal of culture is once again the language of everyday life. And this reinforces the conviction (itself much older than postmodernism) that art is a matter of common human concerns, and that there is something self-contradictory in talking about common concerns in uncommon language.

This is obviously a mistake. Questions which are of interest to everyone are not necessarily simple. Lungs and livers are of interest to everyone, but medics discuss them in fairly abstruse ways. They make fine distinctions and portray complex processes of the kind that our everyday language does not require. Moral matters are also of common human concern, but because the question of what it means to live well is a hard one to answer, moral philosophy has had to evolve its specialized forms of speech in order to tackle it. The same goes for talk about neuroses or the political state. As far as neurosis goes, it is interesting that one of the rare bodies of theory to seep down to street level is psychoanalysis. This highly arcane theory, astonishingly, is the common dialect of the street. Terms like 'ego', 'Oedipus complex', 'libido', 'paranoia' and 'unconscious' have become part of everyday language, in a way that 'ideology', 'commodity fetishism' or 'mode of production' have not.

Why this is so merits a study in itself. But it may be partly because there is something bizarre and sensational about the language of psychoanalysis whch captures the popular imagination, as there isn't about the language of Marxism or semiotics. The other striking example of an obscure jargon becoming the common speech of millions is theology. 'Grace', 'sacrament', 'Trinity' and 'original sin' are hardly simple terms, but they are certainly everyday ones. Ordinary people have no difficulty in grasping such complex notions if they seem relevant to their lives, just as they have no problem in deciphering complex economics if their wage packets are at stake.

We are accustomed to issues of general interest being discussed in everyday language. The press is an obvious example. We are also used to issues of minority interest being expressed in specialized language, such as the jargon of pigeon fanciers or sado-masochists. What is more disconcerting is to hear questions of common interest expressed in specialist ways. This is frustrating, since it makes us feel that we ought to be able to understand this language when in fact we don't. Discussing issues of common interest in specialized ways is not a bad description of the role of the classical intellectual. What has happened in our time is that 'cultural theorist' has become a new label for what used to be known as the intellectual. 'Culture' is now one of the main patches on which we can raise the kind of searching, fundamental questions that the intelligentsia at their best have traditionally voiced.

This was not always so. Historically speaking, the role of the intellectual has shifted from one patch to another. Intellectuals had to find the sort of specific language in which more general, fundamental issues of humanity could be raised. They were in search of what we might call a meta-language – one through which they could have simultaneous access to questions of politics, ethics, metaphysics and the like. And what this might be has altered from time to time and place to place. Sometimes one academic subject has provided intellectuals with a temporary home, and sometimes another. Sooner or later, they tended to find themselves being rudely evicted and in search of alternative accommodation.

Once upon a time, it was theology – the so-called queen of the humanities – where the intellectual pitched his tent. Theology conveniently linked ethics, politics, aesthetics, metaphysics, everyday life and ultimate truth. This arrangement came to an end when theology became the queen of the humanities in a rather less reputable sense of the word. For a time, then, it was philosophy which gave the intellectual house room – indeed, it still is in those European cultures for which philosophy has not been reduced to an aridly semantic affair. For the nineteenth century, the obvious place for the intellectual to be was in science. The natural sciences were now the paradigm of human knowledge, with implications far beyond the nature of the physical world. Science spread its influence into ethics, sociology, theology, philosophy, literature and the like, and so was the kind of busy crossroads where the intellectual could take up home. If Voltaire and Rousseau were typical intellectuals of the eighteenth century, Darwin and Huxley played that role to perfection in the century that followed. But the nineteenth century also saw the rise of the so-called man of letters, whose task was to move between a number of specialized fields of knowledge, judging them from a broadly moral, socially responsible, humanistic standpoint. This kind of well-informed dilettante had to be proficient in more than one subject if he or she was to earn a living as a reviewer. The nineteenth century also witnessed the growth of the new disciplines of sociology and anthropology, which promised to provide meta-languages of a kind.

It is here that the essence of the classical intellectual is to be found. Intellectuals were not simply narrow specialists. Indeed, a snap definition of intellectuals might be that they are the opposite of academics. Jean-Paul Sartre deemed a nuclear scientist to be an intellectual only if he or she had signed a petition against nuclear testing. Intellectuals were concerned with the bearing of ideas on society and humanity as a whole. Because they were engaged with fundamental social, political and metaphysical questions, they had to be adept in more than one academic arena. What academic label, for example, could be pinned on writers like Raymond Williams, Susan Sontag, Jurgen Habermas, Julia Kristeva or Michel Foucault? There is no obvious term to describe the kind of thinkers they are, which is one reason why the rather vague word 'theory' floated into existence. And the fact that their work cannot easily be categorized is a central part of its significance.

Yet there was a clear danger of amateurism here. As knowledge grew more complex and technical, there was a need for thinkers who could shake off their scholarly myopia and address some unsettling questions to society as a whole. Indeed, some of these questions concerned the very forces which were creating this division of intellectual labour in the first place. Yet in a world of jealously compartmentalized knowledges, where was such a figure to stand? And what would he or she have to say that would be of relevance? Would they not have to stand so far back that their speech sank to an inaudible murmur? How could a discourse which assaulted the division of intellectual labour itself be intellectually legitimate?

There were, in short, fewer and fewer vacancies for sages, prophets, peripatetic moralists, belle-lettrists, cracker-barrel phil-osophers and Meaning-of-the-Universe merchants. This was in one sense an advance. It was a relief to be hectored no longer by the authoritarian rant of men like Thomas Carlyle, or patronized by the bland generalities of a Matthew Arnold. But the situation was also highly convenient for a social order which had no particular eagerness to be fundamentally challenged. Intellectuals now had to find some way of launching such challenges without falling back into the blithe amateurism of the gentleman scholar on the one hand, or capitulating to the short-sighted scholars on the other. They were caught between dons and dilettantes, at ease with neither. They were too scornful of traditional academic specialisms for the dons, but their language was too technical for the dilettantes. And they were too politically involved for either camp to feel comfortable with.

From the late nineteenth century onward, the role of the intellectual came to pass more and more to the humanities. There were several reasons for this transition. In a world dominated by science and commerce, the humanities were being pushed increasingly to the margins; but this lent them the powerfully distancing perspective on the social order which was not so available to those in the thick of its commercial, scientific and technological interests. Ironically, then, it was their growing superfluousness in a philistine society which lent the humanities a new kind of spiritual centrality. It was just that, for much the same reasons, they were unlikely to be attended to.

Besides, the humanities, or 'culture', was one place where the crisis of modernity as a whole was most sensitively registered. Culture was about civility, community, imaginative creation, spiritual values, moral qualities, the texture of lived experience, all of which were under siege from a soulless industrial capitalism. Science, philosophy and sociology all seemed to have capitulated to this barbarous order. Philosophy appeared too fascinated by the logical distinction between the phrases 'nothing matters' and 'nothing chatters' to take much interest in changing the world. Moral thought assumed that enlightened self-interest was the driving force of human life. Sociology investigated society as it was, not as it might be. It looked as though culture, *faute de mieux*, was left holding the buck.

Now that religion was on the wane, culture seemed the only forum where one could still raise questions about fundamental ends and values, in the midst of a society impatient with such airy-fairy notions. If culture could be critical, however, it was partly because of its increasing irrelevance. It could be permitted its toothless dissent. Many of its solutions to contemporary woes were backward-looking, patrician and intolerably high-minded, which served to underline its pathos. Like religion, it was often enough valued in theory but disregarded in practice. Culture was what you tipped your hat to on the way to the bank. It was therefore just the place for the intellectual – a figure who retained a certain venerable spiritual aura, but whom nobody took very seriously when it came to working out where to locate the new sewage plant. Like culture, intellectuals were inside and outside society at the same time. They had authority but not power. They were the secular clergy of the modern age.

But there was a more positive reason for the growing appeal of culture to the intelligentsia. If they needed to avoid the kidgloved gentleman-scholar on the one hand and the horny-handed specialist on the other, culture seemed to be just the way to do it. On the one hand, no concept could be more general. In fact, one of its embarrassments was that it was hard to know what it left out. It ranged all the way from the rarefied peaks of art to the humdrum valleys of everyday life. Chopin was culture, and so was double-entry book-keeping. On the other hand, culture was becoming an increasingly specialist set of pursuits – no longer just an abstract idea but a whole industry, which demanded some toughly analytical investigation. If culture could pronounce on the quality of social life as a whole, it could also come up with detailed accounts of working-class hair-styles or the strategies of Expressionism. It combined scope and specificity. If it had the open texture of a social concept, it also had the close-grainedness of an aesthetic one. As such, it had a natural allure for intellectuals, not least because it now seemed hard to raise the kind of questions which concerned them from within an increasingly co-opted politics, economics, sociology and philosophy. The intellectual, accordingly, became the cultural theorist. Culture was left holding the baby partly because those around it had cut and run.

The sense that there was something self-contradictory about

the idea of cultural theory, however, would not go away. It was all very well to intellectualize about politics or economics, since these seemed to be properly impersonal matters. As such, they lent themselves to a clinical, dispassionate treatment. Culture, however, was the very home of value, passion, sensuous experience, more concerned with how the world felt than with how it was. It was not the kind of thing to be cerebral and cold-blooded about. Intellectuals had long been seen in Anglo-Saxon cultures as desiccated, buttoned-down life-deniers, but also as sinisterly robotic and remote. One thinks of the spooky opening music of the TV show *Mastermind*, as opposed to the jolly student jingle of *University Challenge*. There is something spine-chilling about the intellect. A history of Western rationalism has severed it from the emotions, leaving it menacingly frigid and unfeeling. Intellectuals are the thin-lipped Robespierres of Anglo-Saxon nightmare. Would a theorist even recognize an artistic emotion, let alone have anything to say about it?

Yet the popular image of intellectuals is in fact hopelessly confused. If they are censured as cold-hearted, they are also denounced as passionately partisan. Indeed, from a conservative point of view they combine the worst of both worlds. On the one hand, they turn a stonily distancing gaze on the customs and pieties dear to traditionalist hearts; on the other hand, they are associated with rancour, polemic and partisanship. If they are steely-eyed and grim of visage, they are also wild-haired and comically shambolic. As such, they are an odd mixture of clowns and clinicians, to be mocked as much as feared.

The contradiction, however, is only apparent. It is just because intellectuals seek to examine customs and pieties, rather than complacently take them for granted, that they are stirred to clamour for social change. Detaching yourself from received pieties like the need to slap down hard on trade unionists goes along with a passion for a society in which working people are treated less as disposable commodities. Radical intellectuals are not without passion, just without conservative passions. If you try to look dispassionately at the overall structure of society, you might well end up being fired by the conviction that it stands in need of a major overhaul. The dispassionate and the partisan are not necessarily at loggerheads. Popular prejudice is right to see the classical intellectual as both together, even if it has precious little idea why.

It is odd to dismiss cultural intellectuals as cerebral, emotionally anaemic creatures when they are to be found at work these days on madness, fantasy, sado-masochism, horror films, eroticism, pornography and schizoid poetry. Some people find these topics trashy, but only seriously bizarre people find them tediously cerebral. In any case, studying flower imagery in Alfred Tennyson is not exactly a Dionysian pursuit. What the critics of such cultural theory miss is its sheer excitement. It is this, above all, which has attracted generations of students to it, along with the belief that it raises fundamental questions which are too often ducked by conventional criticism. Critics of theory sometimes complain that its devotees seem to find theory more exciting than the works of art it is meant to illuminate. But sometimes it is. Freud is a lot more fascinating than Cecil Day Lewis. Foucault's *The Order of Things* is a good deal more arresting and original than the novels of Charles Kingsley.

The assumption that theory is valuable only if it illuminates works of art is an interesting one. Somewhere behind it lurks the puritanical conviction that anything which is not useful, which has no immediate cash-value, is a form of sinful self-indulgence. Everything from thinking to love-making must justify its existence before some grim-lipped tribunal of utility. Even our thoughts must be rigorously instrumental. There is no recognition here of Bertolt Brecht's desire that thinking might become 'a real sensuous pleasure'. Unless thinking is directly tied to doing, it is worthless. It is hard to see how you could justify astronomy on these grounds. The political left has its own version of this philistine pragmatism, in the assumption that 'theory' must always be directly geared to 'practice'. Gazing at a Jackson Pollock is permissible only if it makes a tangible contribution to the emancipation of the working class.

It is true that theory can powerfully illuminate works of art. (Though some of those who pretend to regard this as its sole justification in fact doubt that it can.) But it can also be richly illuminating in its own right. Not a single branch of cultural theory – feminism, structuralism, psychoanalysis, Marxism, semiotics and the like – is in principle confined to the discussion of art, or actually began life there. This, for some of its critics, is quite enough to disqualify it. They forget that this is also true of much so-called traditional criticism. ('So-called', because the narrow conception of criticism as purely 'aesthetic' is not in fact traditional at all. Our current ideas of the aesthetic are themselves of recent vintage. Criticism began life in ancient society as rhetoric, which was always diverse in its uses and political in its effects.) It is true that in a social order which urgently needs repair, theory must indeed be harnessed to practical political ends. But we would know that a social order had improved in this respect when we no longer felt the compulsion to justify our thinking at the bar of utility. We would then be able to think for its own sake, without feeling the neurotic impulse to apologize for it. We would see that Freud, for example, is worth reading for his own sake, not just to throw light on *Where the Wild Things Are*.

Cultural theory is in the habit of posing what one might call meta-questions. Instead of asking 'Is this poem valuable?' it asks 'What do we mean by calling a poem good or bad?' Instead of asking whether the novel has an implausible plot, it asks itself what a novel is anyway. Instead of asking whether the clarinet concerto is slightly too cloying to be entirely persuasive, it inquires about the material conditions which you need to produce concertos in the first place, and how these help to shape the work itself. Critics discuss symbols, whereas theorists ask by what mysterious process one thing can come to stand for another. Critics talk about the character of Coriolanus, while theorists ask how it comes about that a pattern of words on a page can appear to be a person.

None of these meta-questions need *replace* straightforward critical questions. You can ask both kinds of question together. But theory, in its unassuming way, is unsettled by the way in which conventional art criticism seems to take far too much briskly for granted. It moves too fast and self-assuredly, refusing to push questions far back enough. It has the air of appearing to know all kinds of things that we are actually unsure about. In this sense, theory is less dogmatic than conventional criticism, more agnostic and open-minded. It wants to take fewer preconceptions casually for granted, and to scrutinize our spontaneous assumptions as far as it can. Inquiry, of course, has to begin somewhere. In principle, it is possible to push the question back *ad infinitum*. But received ways of talking about culture are rather too precipitous in what they take as read.

From this viewpoint, non-theorists look remarkably lacking in curiosity. Though they may have been studying, say, prose fiction for years, they never seem to have paused to ask themselves what prose fiction actually is. It would be like caring for an animal for years without having a clue whether it was a badger, a rabbit or a deformed mongoose. This is not to assume that there is only one answer, or even any satisfactory answer at all, to the question of what fiction is. It is just to propose that the question is worth asking.

One might begin to answer it by pointing out that fiction is a kind of writing in which you can neither lie, tell the truth nor make a mistake. You cannot lie in fiction, because the reader does not assume that you are intending to be truthful. 'Once upon a time, there was a little girl called Goldilocks' is not true, but it is not a lie either. 'Oh no, there wasn't' is not a relevant riposte, even though it is a true one. Lying means stating what is false with an intention to deceive, and nobody is out to con us that Goldilocks really existed. 'Refreshes the parts that other beers can't reach' is not true, but neither is it a lie, since nobody is expected to take such a palpable exaggeration literally. 'Once upon a time, there was a little girl called Goldilocks' can always be rewritten: 'I invite you to imagine a fictional world in which there was a little girl called Goldilocks.' Even if there did happen to be a little girl called Goldilocks, who actually did meet up with three bears, this would not affect the fictional status of the story. The story is not there to give us factual information, but to deliver what one might call a moral truth. The fact that this truth in the case of 'Goldilocks' is fairly trivial and blatantly ideological – don't tamper with other people's private property, even if they are hairy, irascible and waddle along on four legs – makes no difference to this fact.

In another sense, to be sure, fiction can be truer than real life, which sometimes gets things hopelessly confused or just plain wrong. It was obtuse of real life to have Byron die of a fever in Greece rather than be felled by a bullet in the fight for Greek independence. It was careless of history to allow the quintessentially Victorian Florence Nightingale to linger on well into the twentieth century, or to allow Robert Maxwell to slip gently into the ocean and escape public disgrace. Art would have handled all of these things much more proficiently.

In another sense, however, fiction is incapable of telling the truth. If an author breaks off to assure us that what she is now asserting is actually true – that it really, literally happened – we would take this as a fictional statement. Novelists and short-story writers are like the boy who cried wolf: they are condemned to be perpetually disbelieved. You could put the statement in a separate footnote and sign it with your initials and the date, but this would not transfer it from fiction to fact. The subtitle 'A Novel' is enough to ensure that. In his novel *Doctor Faustus*, Thomas Mann pauses to pay homage to a real-life individual, a man whose actual existence we might well take his word for. But there is still nothing to stop us from choosing to take this reference fictionally. Even if a novel states actual facts, it does not somehow become truer. Once again, the fact that we know this is a novel ensures that we do not scrutinize these statements for their truth-value, but take them as part of some overall rhetorical design. Novels do not exist to tell us that the loris is a slow-moving nocturnal primate or that Helena is the capital of Montana. They mobilize such facts as part of a moral pattern.

It is hard for fiction to make mistakes, because one of the invisible instructions which accompanies it is: 'Take everything said here as intended.' If an author makes Napoleon an adolescent girl, we assume that this is not just the result of shockingly negligent educators. If she consistently misspells Napoleon's name, we assume that this, too, has some kind of symbolic significance. If she misspells his name only once or twice, we might well assume that this is a typo, and so no part of the literary text itself. Fiction, in short, is an ideal form for those with only a fragile grasp of the factual world. Nobody can unmask their ignorance. This is one reason why there is an intimate bond between otherworldly intellectuals and creative writers, who occasionally inhabit the same body.

The opponents of theory may feel that raising questions of this kind is sinister, robotic, stony-hearted and outrageously partisan. Others may feel that it is actually quite interesting. Take, for example, the difference between poetry and prose. The only satisfactory way of describing this difference is that in poetry it is the author who decides where the lines end, whereas in prose it is the typesetter. To find out why this is the only adequate way of describing the difference between the two forms – why the more obvious apparent differences will not really do – you have to read some theory.

Or think of the question of how much a reader brings to a literary work, and how much the work provides itself. Take, for example, the unbeatably comic first sentence of Evelyn Waugh's short story 'Mr Loveday's Little Outing': '"You will not find your father greatly changed," remarked Lady Moping as the car turned into the gates of the County Asylum.' This is really a form of English irony, bringing the momentous (insanity) and the everyday off-handedly together. The stiff upper lip lurks somewhere behind this comic device, as the grotesque or catastrophic is taken impassively on the chin.

Waugh's sentence, however, is also a fine example of English understatement. As such, it reminds us just how understated all literature is, even at its most luridly melodramatic. It illustrates how the reader of a literary work unconsciously supplies information which is needed to make sense of it, or makes vital assumptions which may not be entirely warranted. We assume that Lady Moping is talking to a child of hers sitting alongside her in the car, who is also the offspring of an inmate of the asylum whom they are about to visit. We also probably assume that the inmate in question is Lady Moping's husband – presumably Lord Moping.

None of this, however, is actually stated. We will, of course, discover the truth of the matter as we read on, but we can still enjoy the laconic comedy of the opening sentence simply by making certain assumptions. If we assume that the father in question is indeed Lady Moping's husband, the comic edge of her callous nonchalance is notably sharpened. The humour only really works if we assume that the father is an inmate of the asylum, though this is pure conjecture. It may be that Lady Moping simply happens to mention him while visiting the asylum for some other purpose, or that he is indeed in the building but one of the medical staff. That the father is not greatly changed amusingly suggests that he was as mad as a hatter when on the loose, though it could be Lady Moping's way of reassuring his son or daughter that despite his incarceration he is as sweetly reasonable as he always was. The syntax of the sentence ('as the car turned . . .') hints at the shadowy presence of a chauffeur, Lady Moping being too grand to drive herself, though this, too, is readerly inference.

It is a shame to ruin a good joke with too much theory. But finding out what it takes for comedy to work is an interesting business. One might note that doing this has just involved a spot of reasonably close reading, of the kind which theorists are said to be incapable of performing. That theory is incapable of close reading is one of its opponents' most recurrent gripes. It is now almost as received a wisdom as the belief that baldness is incurable or that Naomi Campbell lacks humility. In fact, it is almost entirely false. Some theoretical critics are careless readers, but so are some non-theoretical ones. When it comes to a thinker like Jacques Derrida, the more apt accusation might be that he is far *too* painstaking a reader – that he stands so close up to the work, fastidiously probing its most microscopic features, that like a painting viewed from too near it threatens to disintegrate into a set of streaks and blurs. The same can be said of many other deconstructive writers. As far as most other major theorists go, the charge of standing too far back from the work simply will not stick. Most of them read quite as tenaciously as non-theoretical critics, and some of them rather more so.[1]

The advocates of close analysis sometimes assume that there is an ideal distance to be established between the reader and the work. But this is an illusion. Reading, viewing and listening involve constant focus-changing, as we sometimes swoop in on a stray particular and sometimes pull back to pan the whole. Some readings or viewings approach a work head-on, while others sidle shyly up to it. Some cling to its gradual unfolding as a process in time, while others aim for a snapshot or spatial fix. Some slice into it sideways, while others peer up at it from ground level. There are critics who start off with their noses squashed against the work, soaking up its most primitive first impressions, before gradually stepping backwards to encompass its surroundings. None of these approaches is correct. There is no correctness or incorrectness about it.

A common assumption of the critics of theory is that theory 'gets in between' the critic and the work. It interposes its obtrusive bulk between the two, throwing its ungainly shadow over the words on the page or the shapes on the canvas. It is a thick mesh of doctrine laid across the work, allowing only select bits of it to peep through. Other bits get distorted or blocked

---

1. Some examples: Theodor Adorno on Brecht, Walter Benjamin on Baudelaire, Paul de Man on Proust, Fredric Jameson on Conrad, Julia Kristeva on Mallarmé, Geoffrey Hartman on Wordsworth, Roland Barthes on Balzac, Franco Moretti on Goethe, Harold Bloom on Stevens, J. Hillis Miller on Henry James. The list could be greatly extended.

out. Moreover, the same mesh is laid monotonously across every work which comes along, destroying their uniqueness and erasing their differences. It is true that some criticism behaves in this way, but not all of it is theoretical. The belle-lettristic gentlemen who ran the critical show some decades ago certainly wielded such a doctrinal filter. Bits of art concerned with gender or class conflict got regularly blocked out, while negative criticism of great authors was felt to be discourteous. The social context of art was admitted only in a highly filleted fashion. The same fulsome vocabulary – 'remarkably fine', 'splendidly robust', 'drearily naturalistic', 'sublimely accomplished' – was ruthlessly superimposed on every work. The prejudices of the patrician class clumsily obtruded themselves between the reader and the work.

In fact, the whole idea of a critical language 'interposing' itself between the reader and the work is a misleading spatial metaphor. Some critical commentaries are indeed unhelpful, but this is not the best way of seeing why. Without preconceptions of some sort, we would not even be able to identify a work of art in the first place. Without some sort of critical language at our disposal we would simply not know what to look for, just as there is no point in introspection if we have no vocabulary in which to identify what we find inside ourselves. The wholly disinterested view of a work, one which did not come at it from a specific angle, would be struck blind. It would be completely at a loss, like a visitor from Alpha Centauri confronted with *The Simpsons*.

At their most useful, critical concepts are what allow us access to works of art, not what block them off from us. They are ways of getting a handle on them. Some of them may be more effective handles than others, but that distinction does not map on to the difference between theory and non-theory. A critical concept, even a useless or obfuscatory one, is not a screen which slams down between ourselves and the work of art. It is a way of trying to do things with it, some of which work and some of which do not. At its best, it picks out certain features of the work so that we can situate it within a significant context. And different concepts will disclose different features. Theorists are pluralists in this respect: there could be no set of concepts which opened up the work for us in its entirety. The key difference is between those concepts which are so familiar to us that they have become as transparent as words like 'bread', and those which still retain the strangeness of words like 'jujube'. It is the latter which are generally called 'theory', though jujubes are in fact no odder than bread.

What have been cultural theory's achievements? To begin with, it has disabused us of the idea that there is a single correct way to interpret a work of art. There is a joke about the bogusly ecumenical Catholic who conceded to his Protestant colleague that there were many ways of worshipping God, 'you in your way, and I in His'. This is pretty much how many conservative critics regard theorists. They themselves read the work as it would wish to be read could it but speak, whereas theorists perversely insist on importing a lot of fancy ideas into it. To see *The Waste Land* as brooding upon the spiritual vacancy of Man without God is to read what is there on the page, whereas to view it as a symptom of an exhausted bourgeois civilization in an era of imperialist warfare is to impose your own crankish theory on the poem. To speak of spiritual exploration in D. H. Lawrence is to be true to the texts, while to speak of sexism in his work is to twist them to your own political purposes.

To read *Wuthering Heights* as a novel about death is to respond to what is there before you, whereas to read it as a novel about the death drive is to let Freud come between you and Heathcliff. Jane Austen is about love, marriage and moral values; only those deaf to the claims of the heart see all this as inseparable in her novels from property and social class. To read Philip Larkin straight is to appreciate his wry regret for the passing of pastoral England, whereas to read him between ideological blinkers is to see his poetry as part of a jaded post-imperial Britain.

To acknowledge that *King Lear* has more than one meaning is not to claim that it can mean anything at all. Theorists do not hold that anything can mean anything; it is just that their reasons why it cannot differ somewhat from other accounts. It is only authoritarians who fear that the only alternative to their own beliefs is no beliefs at all, or any belief you like. Like anarchists, they see chaos all around them; it is just that the anarchist regards this chaos as creative, whereas they regard it as menacing. The authoritarian is just the mirror-image of the nihilist. Whereas true meaning is neither carved in stone nor a free-for-all, neither absolutist nor laissez-faire. You have to be able to pick out features of the work of art which will support your interpretation of it. But there are many different such features, interpretable in different ways; and what counts as a feature is itself open to argument. No critical hypothesis is impregnable; all of them are revisable.

What other achievements has cultural theory to its credit? It has persuaded us that there are many things involved in the making of a work of art besides the author. Works of art have a kind of 'unconscious', which is not under the control of their producers. We have come to understand that one of those producers is the reader, viewer or listener – that the recipient of a work of art is a co-creator of it, without whom it would not exist. We have become more sensitive to the play of power and desire in cultural artefacts, to the variety of ways in which they can confirm or contest political authority. We understand, too, that this is at least as much a matter of their form as of their content. A sharper sense has emerged of how intimately works of culture belong to their specific times and places – and how this can enrich rather than diminish them. The same is true of our responses to them, which are always historically specific. Closer attention has been paid to the material contexts of such art-works, and of how so much culture and civility have had their roots in unhappiness and exploitation. We have come to recognize culture in the broader sense as an arena in which the discarded and dispossessed can explore shared meanings and affirm a common identity.

Of all these gains, one of the most controversial has been the link between culture and power. The point about culture for the liberal or conservative is that it is the very opposite of power. Indeed, it is one of those blessed, beleaguered places where we can still escape power's unlovely sway. As social life fell increasingly under the rule of utility, culture was on hand to remind us that there were things which had value but no price. As a crassly instrumental reason tightened its grip on human affairs, culture rejoiced in whatever existed purely for its own sake, with no end in sight but its own abundant self-delight. It bore witness to the profundity of play, in contrast to the burdensome yoke of labour. As human life became increasingly quantified and administered, art was there to press the claims of the uniquely individual. It recalled us to our bodily, sensuous existence in a world where even this was being relentlessly commodified.

In all these ways, culture has acted as a precious remembrance of utopia. As art became less and less integral to a civilization for which value was whatever the market declared it to be, it was able to turn this very non-necessity into a kind of virtue. It could speak up for the contingent, the stray particular, the gloriously pointless, the miraculous exception, in a world of iron laws and inexorable forces. Indeed, it could illustrate this contingency by seizing on the miracle of its own stubbornly persistent existence, in a society to which it mattered less and less. Because it had less and less identifiable function, culture could question the whole brutal assumption that things had to be functional in order to earn their keep. It could act as a political critique simply by being stubbornly faithful to itself.

At the same time, it could take advantage of the fact that it was adrift in society to peer beyond society's provincial limits, exploring issues which were of vital concern to humanity as a whole. It could be universal rather than narrowly historical. It could raise ultimate questions, not just pragmatic, parochial ones. Those who dismiss the universal out of hand forget that this is so often the alternative. Culture could provide a home for all those vagrant values which orthodox society had expelled as so much unproductive garbage: the deviant, the visionary, the erotic, the transcendent. As such, it was a living rebuke to the civilization which had given birth to it – not so much because of what it showed or said, but simply by virtue of its strange, pointless, unnerving presence.

One can understand, then, the fury of those who see cultural theory as seeking to demolish this last bastion of the human spirit. If even this frail citadel of human value can be invaded by power and politics, it is hard to see where else one can retreat to. This was by no means always the case. In the days before culture shifted centre-stage, there was an obvious dwelling place for the spirit, known as religion. Religion did all that culture was later to do, but far more effectively. It could enlist countless millions of men and women in the business of ultimate value, not just the few well-educated enough to read Horace or listen to Mahler. To assist it in this task, it had the threat of hell fire at its disposal – a penalty which proved rather more persuasive than the murmurs of cultivated distaste around those who hadn't read Horace. Religion has been for most of human history one of the most precious components of popular life, even though almost all theorists of popular culture embarrassedly ignore it.

Through ritual and moral code, religion could link questions of absolute value to men and women's everyday experience. Nothing was less abstract than God, heaven, sin, redemption. Just as art fleshes out fundamental issues in sign, sound, paint and stone, so religion brought them home to everyday experience in a whole iconography, devotional sensibility, pattern of personal conduct and set of cultic practices. It planted the cosmic Law in the very depths of the individual, in the faculty known as conscience. Faith bound together the people and the intellectuals, the simple faithful and the clergy, in the most durable of bonds. It could create a sense of common purpose far beyond the capacity of a minority culture. It outlined the grandest narrative of all, known as eschatology. It could interweave art, ritual, politics, ethics, mythology, metaphysics and everyday life, while lending this mighty edifice the sanction of a supreme authority. It was thus a particular shame that it involved a set of beliefs which seemed to many decent, rational people remarkably benighted and implausible.

It is no wonder, then, that culture has been in perpetual crisis since the moment it was thrust into prominence. For it has been called upon to take over these functions in a post-religious age; and it is hardly surprising that for the most part it has lamentably failed to do so. Part of religion's force was to link fact and value, the routine conduct of everyday life with matters of ultimate spiritual importance. Culture, however, divides these domains down the middle. In its broad, popular, everyday sense, it means a set of ways of doing things; in its artistic sense, it means a body of work of fundamental value. But the connection between them is fatally missing. Religion, by contrast, is culture in both senses at once.

To speak of a post-religious age is to speak a good deal too hastily. The age may look that way in Leeds or Frankfurt, but hardly in Dacca or Dallas. It may seem irreligious to intellectuals, but not to peasant farmers or office cleaners. In most stretches of the globe, including much of the United States, culture never ousted religion in the first place. Even in some regions where it did, religion is creeping back with a vengeance. On the planet in general, it is still by far the most resourceful symbolic form. As men and women feel more vulnerable and disregarded, we can expect ugly religious fundamentalisms of various stripes to escalate. The age in which culture sought to play surrogate to religion is perhaps drawing to a close. Perhaps culture, in this respect at least, has finally admitted defeat.

Conservatives are mistaken to believe that radicals are out to rob culture of its political innocence. Like most forms of innocence, it never existed in the first place. In any case, it is radicals and not conservatives who have emphasized the affirmative, utopian dimensions of culture. It is just that they have pointed at the same time to the ways in which it is complicit with unsavoury forms of power. Indeed, these two aspects of culture are not unrelated. By encouraging us to dream beyond the present, it may also provide the existing social order with a convenient safety-valve. Imagining a more just future may confiscate some of the energies necessary to achieve it. What cannot be achieved in reality can be fulfilled in fantasy. In any case, fantasy is far from a stranger to the workings of advanced capitalist orders.

This, however, qualifies the utopian role of culture rather than undermines it. It means simply that culture is utopian in both a positive and a negative sense. If it resists power, it is itself a compelling form of it. The radical view of the matter, in other words, is more pluralistic and open-ended than that of those for whom artistic culture is of unequivocal value; radicals are rather more nuanced and equivocal about the subject. They like to see both sides of the issue. They do not assume, in dogmatically generalizing spirit, that art is always and everywhere positive. They are mindful, for example, of the abuse and exploitation which so often lie at its roots. This does not invalidate art for them; it simply makes their approach to it more tentative and multi-faceted. They are wary of being too sweeping about the matter, in the manner of their liberal humanist colleagues.

Not many of the standard objections to cultural theory that we have examined hold water. Some of it has been intolerably jargon-ridden; but the impulse behind it is attractively democratic, and it has probably produced more fine stylists than its non-theoretical counterpart. Anyway, some forms of specialized language are desirable rather than distasteful. It is not true that cultural theory avoids close reading. It is neither clinical nor cold-blooded. It is not out to abolish the human spirit, but to bring it down to earth. It does not necessarily interpose itself between the art-work and its recipients. If it can sometimes be an obstacle to real understanding, so can other forms of art criticism. It does not believe that Jeffrey Archer is as good as Jane Austen; it simply inquires what we mean when we make such claims.

Most of the objections to theory are either false or fairly trifling. A far more devastating criticism of it can be launched. Cultural theory as we have it promises to grapple with some fundamental problems, but on the whole fails to deliver. It has been shamefaced about morality and metaphysics, embarrassed about love, biology, religion and revolution, largely silent about evil, reticent about death and suffering, dogmatic about essences, universals and foundations, and superficial about truth, objectivity and disinterestedness. This, on any estimate, is rather a large slice of human existence to fall down on. It is also, as we have suggested before, rather an awkward moment in history to find oneself with little or nothing to say about such fundamental questions. Let us see if we can begin to remedy these deficiencies by addressing these issues in a different light.

5

Truth, Virtue and Objectivity

No idea is more unpopular with contemporary cultural theory than that of absolute truth. The phrase smacks of dogmatism, authoritarianism, a belief in the timeless and universal. Let us begin, then, by seeking to defend this remarkably modest, eminently reasonable notion.

It is a mistake to think of absolute truth as a special kind of truth. On this view, there are truths which are changing and relative, and there is a higher kind of truth which is neither. Instead, it is fixed for all eternity. The idea is that some people, usually those of a dogmatic or authoritarian turn of mind, believe in this higher kind of truth, while others, such as historicists and postmodernists, do not. In fact, some postmodernists claim not to believe in truth at all – but this is just because they have identified truth with dogmatism, and in rejecting dogmatism have thrown out truth along with it. This is a peculiarly pointless manoeuvre. In less sophisticated postmodern circles, holding a position with conviction is seen as unpleasantly authoritarian, whereas to be fuzzy, sceptical and ambiguous is somehow democratic. It is hard in that case to know what to say about someone who is passionately committed to democracy, as opposed to someone who is fuzzy and ambiguous about it.

For this strain of postmodernism, claiming that one position is preferable to another is objectionably 'hierarchical'. It is not clear on this theory why being anti-hierarchical is preferable to being hierarchical. A certain postmodern fondness for not knowing what you think about anything is perhaps reflected in the North American speech habit of inserting the word 'like' after every three or four words. It would be dogmatic to suggest that something actually *is* what it is. Instead, you must introduce a ritual tentativeness into your speech, in a kind of perpetual semantic slurring.

People who see truth as dogmatic, and so want no truck with it, are rather like people who call themselves immoralists because they believe that morality just means forbidding people to go to bed with each other. Such people are inverted puritans. Like the puritan, they equate morality with repression; to live a moral life is to have a terrible time. But whereas the puritan thinks that having a terrible time is an excellent thing, and remarkably character-building to boot, these people do not, and so reject morality altogether. Similarly, those who do not believe in truth are quite often inverted dogmatists. They reject an idea of truth that no reasonable person would defend in the first place.

There is not, in fact, a class of mundane, historically changeable truths, along with a superior class of absolute truths which you may believe in or not, as some people believe in angels and some do not. Some statements are true only from particular viewpoints: a celebrated example is 'France is hexagonal', which is true only for those who look at the world from within a specific geometric framework. But there are lots of other truths which are absolute, without being in any sense lofty or superior.[1] 'This fish tastes a

1. For an excellent defence of the notion of truth as absolute, see Paul O'Grady, *Relativism*, Chesham, Bucks, 2002, ch. 2. See also Bernard Williams, *Truth and Truthfulness*, Princeton and Oxford, 2002, p. 258f.

bit off', if it is true, is just as absolutely true as 'I say unto you, before Abraham was, I am' claims to be. That truths of this kind are absolute is of no great moment. It simply means that if a statement is true, then the opposite of it can't be true at the same time, or true from some other point of view. It can't be the case that the fish is both a bit off and not a bit off. It can't be fresh for you and putrid for me, even if putrid is the way I like it. This does not rule out the possibility of doubt or ambiguity. Maybe I am not sure whether the fish is off or not. But if I'm not sure, it is absolutely true that I am not sure. I can't be sure and not sure at the same time. It can't be that I am sure from my point of view but not from yours. Maybe the fish was fine two hours ago and is now distinctly dubious. In that case, what was absolutely true two hours ago is no longer true now. And the fact that it is not true now is just as absolute.

'Absolutely true', here, really just means 'true'. We could drop the 'absolute' altogether, were it not for the need to argue against relativists who insist, as their name implies, that truth is relative. Not many relativists are rash enough to claim that 'I am now in Damascus' and 'I am now in Doncaster' could both be true if spoken by the same person at the same moment in time. They are more likely to suggest that the same proposition could be true for you but not for me, or true on Monday but not on Friday, or true for the Flemish but not for the Azande. As far as many truths go, however, not much of this is very convincing. What is true of you is also true for me. If it is true that you are feeling dispirited while I am feeling ecstatic, then it is true for me that you are feeling dispirited. If you were feeling liverish on Monday but feel fine by Friday, it is still true on Friday that you were feeling liverish on Monday.

Nothing of world-shaking significance is at stake here. There is nothing loudly authoritarian in progress. That truth is absolute simply means that if something *is* established as true – a taxing, messy business, often enough, and one which is always open to revision – then there are no two ways about it. It does not mean that truth can only be discovered from some disinterested viewpoint. In fact, it says nothing about *how* we arrive at truth. It simply says something about the nature of truth itself. All truths are established from specific viewpoints; but it does not make sense to say that there is a tiger in the bathroom from my point of view but not from yours. You and I may contend fiercely about whether there is a tiger in the bathroom or not. To call truth absolute here is just to say that one of us has to be wrong.

If it is true that racism is an evil, then it is not just true for those who happen to be its victims. They are not just expressing how they feel; they are making a statement about the way things are. 'Racism is an evil' is not the same kind of proposition as 'I always find the smell of fresh newsprint blissful.' It is more like the statement 'There is a tiger in the bathroom.' One could imagine someone murmuring consolingly to the victims of racism that he understands just why they feel the way they do; that this feeling is of course entirely valid for them – indeed, that if he were in their shoes he would doubtless feel just the same way; but that in fact he is not in their shoes, and so does not consider the situation to be racist at all. This individual is known as a relativist. He might conceivably be known, less politely, as a racist. Perhaps he might seek to pile on the consolation by adding that the situation at the moment may well be racist, but that in a few years' time those on the sticky end of it will look back and see that it was not racist at all. This is not just cold comfort; it is utterly incoherent.

If it is true that a situation is racist, then it is absolutely true. It is not just my opinion, or yours. But of course it may not be true. Or it may be partially true – in which case it absolutely *is* partially true, as opposed to being completely true or not true at all. Defenders of absolute truth are not necessarily dogmatists. In any case, dogmatism does just not mean thumping the table with one hand and clutching your opponent by the throat with the other. It means refusing to give grounds for your beliefs, appealing instead simply to authority. There are plenty of courteous, soft-spoken dogmatists. Holding something to be absolutely true does not mean affirming it against all conceivable evidence and argument, and refusing in any circumstances to concede that you are mistaken. Those who believe in absolute truth may well be the kind of people who are pathologically cautious about accepting anything as true unless it seems plainly undeniable. They may stumble through life in a haze of scepticism and a miasma of doubt. It is just that when they do, perhaps once every decade or so, come grudgingly to accept a proposition such as 'The head gardener has just shot himself through the foot' as true, they recognize that its opposite cannot also be true, and that its being true for them means its being true for everyone else as well.

Nor does 'absolutely true' mean true independently of any context. We can only judge the world from within some kind of framework. But this does not necessarily mean that what is true from one viewpoint is false from another. Elephants may be sacred for you but not for me, if this represents a difference between our ways of signifying them. But it cannot be true that elephants really are sacred, in the same way that they really have four legs, and that they are in the same sense not sacred. Cultures make sense of the world in different ways, and what some see as a fact others do not; but if truth simply means truth-for-us, then there can be no conflict between us and other cultures, since truth is equally just truth-for-them. This is tolerable enough when it comes to the sacred status of elephants, as well as being extremely convenient for us if we hold that forcing sexual relations on toddlers contributes to their emotional well-being and psychological stability in later years, and the culture next door does not. Since their view is entirely relative to their own way of life, it can naturally have no effect on our behaviour. In any case, if each cultural framework constructs the world differently enough, it is hard to see how they could share the same proposition in common. A different world yields a different meaning.

Absolute truth has nothing to do with fanaticism. It does not necessarily mean the kind of truth to which you are fervently committed. 'Erlangen is in Germany' is absolutely true, but one would not go to one's death for it. It is not the kind of truth which sets the blood coursing and quickens the heartbeat. It does not have the same emotional force as 'You strangled my great-aunt, you despicable bastard!' Most absolute truths are pretty trivial. Much the same goes for the word 'absolute' when used in some moral discourse. For Thomas Aquinas, 'absolutely wrong' does not necessarily mean 'very, very wrong'. The word 'absolute' here is not an intensifier. It just means 'shouldn't be done under any circumstances'. Aquinas thought rather strangely that lying was absolutely wrong, but not killing; but he did not of course believe that lying was always more grievous an offence than killing. Being of reasonable intelligence, he appreciated well enough that lying is sometimes pretty harmless. It was just that for him it was absolutely wrong.

Absolute truth is not truth removed from time and change. Things that are true at one time can cease to be true at another, or new truths can emerge. The claim that some truth is absolute is a claim about what it means to call something true, not a denial that there are different truths at different times. Absolute truth does not mean non-historical truth: it does not mean the kind of truths which drop from the sky, or which are vouchsafed to us by some bogus prophet from Utah. On the contrary, they are truths which are discovered by argument, evidence, experiment, investigation. A lot of what is taken as (absolutely) true at any given time will no doubt turn out to be false. Most apparently watertight scientific hypotheses have turned out to be full of holes. Not everything which is considered to be true is actually true. But it remains the case that it cannot just be raining from my viewpoint.

Why does any of this matter? It matters, for one thing, because it belongs to our dignity as moderately rational creatures to know the truth. And that includes knowing the truth about truth. It is best not to be deceived if we can possibly help it. But it also matters because a ludicrous bugbear has been made of the word 'absolute' in this context; and because if the relativist is right, then truth is emptied of much of its value. As Bernard Williams points out, relativism is really a way of explaining away conflict.[2] If you maintain that democracy means everyone being allowed to vote, while I maintain it means that only those people may vote who have passed a set of fiendishly complicated intelligence tests, there will always be a liberal on hand to claim that we are both right from our different points of view. If true loses its force, then political radicals can stop talking as though it is unequivocally true that women are oppressed or that the planet is being gradually poisoned by corporate greed. They may still want to insist that logic is a ruling-class conspiracy, but they cannot logically expect anyone to believe them. The champions of Enlightenment are right: truth indeed exists. But so are their counter-Enlightenment critics: there is indeed truth, but it is monstrous.

*

2. See Bernard Williams, *Ethics and the Limits of Philosophy*, Cambridge, Mass., 1985, p. 156.

If absolute truth is out of favour these days, so is the idea of objectivity. Perhaps we can begin the rehabilitation of this idea by considering it first in relation to the question of human well-being. All men and women are in pursuit of well-being, but the problem lies in knowing what this consists in. Perhaps it means something different for everybody, or for every period and culture. It is because what counts as well-being is far from clear that we need elaborate discourses like moral and political philosophy to help unravel it. If we were transparent to ourselves, there might be no need for these esoteric ways of talking. We might be able to know what it was to live well just by looking into ourselves, or simply by instinct.

This is the enviable situation of toads, who know by instinct how to do what it is best for toads to do. They simply follow their toad-like nature, and for them to do this is for them to prosper. It is to be a good toad rather than a bad one, living a fulfilling, toad-like existence. Good toads are very toad-like. This is not the kind of goodness you can congratulate them on, however, since being toad-like is something they can't help being. It is not an achievement. Toads do not win medals for being toads. You can have a good toad, but not a virtuous one. On one view, however (not the most popular view today, especially among cultural theorists), human beings have to work fairly hard to become human beings, and so can indeed be congratulated on being human. Because we are able to be false to our natures, there is some virtue in our being true to them.

It may be, then, that we resemble toads in the sense that we, too, have a nature, in the sense of a way of living which is peculiar to being a successful human, and which, if we are true to it, will allow us to prosper. It is just that we are not sure what it is. Or perhaps it changes from one time to another. Because we are linguistic animals, our nature, if we have one at all, is far more tractable and complicated than that of toads. Because of language and labour, and the cultural possibilities they bring in their wake, we can transform what we are in ways that non-linguistic animals cannot. To discover what we are, to know our own natures, we have to think hard about it; and the result is that we have come up over the centuries with a bewildering array of versions of what it is to be human. Or, if you like, what it is for a human animal, as opposed to a slug or a daisy, to live well and to flourish. The history of moral philosophy is littered with rusting, abandoned models of the good life.

Take, for instance, the notion of happiness. To believe that happiness is what human beings are after – that this is the name for their particular mode of living well – is very persuasive. It would explain most of what we see going on around us, from people rising promptly at some unearthly hour of the morning to assiduously drying their toothbrushes at night. But what *is* happiness? If it means simple contentment, then human beings can presumably be happy slumped sluggishly in front of the television set for fourteen hours a day, glazedly munching great fistfuls of potentially lethal substances. It is hard to avoid the suspicion that living a good human life might involve a touch more than this. It sounds too much like being happy in the way a rabbit might be happy.

Does this mean, then, that the glazed munchers are not really happy? Perhaps so, if happiness involves more than sluggish contentment. People can be grossly self-deceived about themselves, including about whether they are happy. It is possible to be thoroughly miserable and not know it. If a galley slave chained to his oar raises his wind-battered head to croak hoarsely that he can conceive of no more privileged way of serving his emperor, before collapsing again in an exhausted heap, we might just suspect that there is some ideological mystification at work here. Or he may be a masochist who can't believe his luck in having stumbled upon such a sadistic psychopath as his captain. Or his previous situation may have been even worse, and this is paradise in comparison. Or he may just not be able to imagine any fuller sort of life. We would need to ask him again whether he was happy once he had tasted a spot of liberty, ecstatic love and sensational success at some esteemed craft on shore.

Even so, people like the munchers who say they are happy may well be right, at least in one sense of the word. They enjoy what they are doing, have no desire ever to lever themselves out of their armchairs (if that, indeed, remains a practical possibility), and don't have a care in the world. Maybe they are not happy in some deeper sense. At a quick glance, they do not seem to have plumbed the rich depths of human potential. But those depths include miseries as well as ecstasies. There may be different ways of being happy, and this may be one of them.

Besides, people who are brutal and violent can be happy, at least in the sense of feeling content with their lives. Gangsters can reap a lot of job-satisfaction from what they do, not to speak of enjoying themselves on the proceeds. You can gain considerable pleasure from murdering doctors who terminate pregnancies, if you feel that you are acting as an instrument of God's will. Military commanders return to their headquarters after a hard day's massacring the local population, quietly satisfied that they have made the world that little bit safer for freedom. It may be, again, that these people are not happy in some deeper sense. But that does not mean that they are not happy at all – that they actually detest having to murder abortionists or Aboriginals, but have managed to convince themselves otherwise. One should not always let people off the hook with an appeal to ideological self-deception. The wicked can be content with their wickedness, and do well out of it. It is pleasant to read salutary tales of them coming to a sticky end, but fiction is not real life. Henry Fielding has his villains come a cropper, but usually sends out ironic signals that this is only because they are in a novel. In real life they would probably have become prime minister.

If the wicked can be happy, the good are often not. Being virtuous in a predatory world, as with some of Fielding's gullible innocents, probably means that you will be atrociously put upon. In such a society, the innocent need to look sharp for themselves; but then how can they still be innocent? You can be virtuous under torture, refusing to betray your comrades, but you cannot be happy. A martyr is someone who sacrifices his or her own happiness so that others may thrive. You may find this fulfilling, but hardly a matter of felicity. It is not what you would have chosen had the situation not seemed to demand it. A martyr who dies deliriously happy is only questionably a martyr. Martyrs give up their lives because they are the most precious thing they have, not because they are only too eager to die.

Despite all this, there is something in our intuition that human beings were made for more than murder and chip-munching. Take the well-known story about George Best, perhaps the finest footballer in history until alcoholism brought him low. Best the ex-footballer was lounging in a five-star hotel room surrounded by caviar and champagne, with a former Miss World lounging amorously beside him, when a member of the hotel staff entered, weighed down with yet more luxury goods. Gazing down at the supine star, he shook his head sadly and murmured: 'George, where did it all go wrong?'

The joke, of course, is that one would hardly claim that life had gone wrong for a man with such a lavish lifestyle. This is how Best tells the story himself. Yet the hotel worker was right: Best's life *had* gone wrong. He was not doing what it was in him to do.

He was certainly enjoying himself, and might even in some sense have been happy; but he was not *flourishing*. He had failed at what he was supremely equipped to excel at. It is true that his life was probably more pleasurable than it had been in his footballing days, when he was constrained to break off nightclubbing from time to time in order to train. It is not that he had been happier as a footballer in the sense of enjoying himself more, though he managed to enjoy himself enough for a whole league of players even then. Nor is the point that his post-footballing lifestyle actually brought him a great amount of suffering, apparently confirming the Evangelical view that the dissolute always get their comeuppance. It is rather that he had ceased to prosper. His life might have been happy in the sense of being opulent, contented and enjoyable, but it was not going anywhere. The casual greeting 'How's it going?' suggests something morally significant. Best had come unstuck as a human being. Indeed, one suspects that he used to tell this story so gleefully partly as a way of disavowing the fact.

But where *are* human lives supposed to be going? They aren't, after all, like buses or bicycle races; and the idea that life is a series of hurdles which you must leap in order to attain a goal is just the punitive puritan fantasy of scout masters, major-generals and corporation executives. What had come unstuck in Best's life was not that he was no longer achieving, but that he was not fulfilling himself. It was not that he was no longer piling up goals, silver trophies and salary cheques, but that he was not living, if the pun may be excused, at his best. He was not being the kind of person he was able best to be. Indeed, he was actively out to destroy it. The post-footballing 'dissipation', as the sniffier commentators tended to call it, was perhaps a substitute way of trying to achieve. Best was now desperately scrambling from one starlet or bottle to another, in a grotesque parody of winning more and more matches.

Throwing up his football career, even if it was getting difficult to carry it on, could be seen in one sense as a courageous rejection of the success ethic. It was a recognition, however bleary-eyed, that life was not a matter of goals, in every sense of the word. Best was now free to enjoy himself, not live as some kind of self-entrepreneur. In another sense, the frenetic high living was a shadow of exactly that. The emptiness of desire replaced the hollowness of achievement. For both ways of life, the present is fairly valueless. It is just a bridge to the future, which will turn out to be just the same. How Best might genuinely have enjoyed himself would have been by carrying on playing football. It would not have been pleasant all the time, and there would no doubt have been times when he felt discontent; but it would have been how he could best thrive. Playing football would have been the moral thing to do.

Perhaps what helped to bring Best down was the fact that he was not able to play football just for its own sake. No footballer can, in a sports industry which is about shareholders rather than players, artistry or spectators. It would be like a hard-pressed commercial designer imagining that he could live like Michelangelo. To live a really fulfilling life, we have to be allowed to do what we do just for the sake of it. Best was no longer able to play just for the delight of it, and turned instead from delight to pleasure. His hedonism was just the other side of the instrumentalism he chafed at.

The point about human nature is that it does not have a goal. In this, it is no different from any other animal nature. There is no point to being a badger. Being a giraffe does not get you anywhere. It is just a matter of doing your giraffe-like things for the sake of it. Because, however, human beings are by nature historical creatures, we look as though we are going somewhere – so that it is easy to misread this movement in teleological terms and forget that it is all for its own sake. Nature is a bottom-line concept: you cannot ask why a giraffe should do the things it does. To say 'It belongs to its nature' is answer enough. You cannot cut deeper than that. In the same way, you cannot ask why people should want to feel happy and fulfilled. It would be like asking what someone hoped to achieve by falling in love. Happiness is not a means to an end.

If someone asks you why you do not want to die, you might reply that you have a trilogy of novels to finish, or grandchildren to watch growing up, or that a shroud would clash horribly with the colour of your fingernails. But it would surely be answer enough to say that you wanted to live. There is no need to specify particular goals. Living is enough reason in itself. There are certainly some people who would be better off dead; but those that would not do not need a reason for carrying on. It is as superfluous to explain why you want to live as it is to explain why you don't enjoy being nuzzled all over by buzzards. The only problem is that something which is or should be valuable in itself, like living, does not seem to need to end. Since it is not instrumental for something else, there is no point at which we can say its function is fulfilled and its purpose over. This is one reason why death is always bound to appear arbitrary. Only a life which had realized itself completely could seem undamaged by it. And as long as we are alive, there is always more self-realization where that came from.

The idea of fulfilling your nature is inimical to the capitalist success ethic. Everything in capitalist society must have its point and purpose. If you act well, then you expect a reward. For Aristotle, by contrast, acting well was a reward in itself. You no more expected a reward for it than you did for enjoying a delectable meal or taking an early morning swim. It is not as though the reward for virtue is happiness; being virtuous *is* to be happy. It is to enjoy the deep sort of happiness which comes from fulfilling your nature. This is not to suggest that the virtuous will always fare well in the world – a doctrine which, as Henry Fielding observes, has only one drawback, namely that it is not true.

You are, in fact, probably more likely to fare well in the world if you are brave, loving, resilient, compassionate, imaginative, resourceful and the like. Other people are less likely to drop iron bars on you from a great height, and even if they do you may have the resourcefulness to dodge them. But the virtuous can of course come unstuck. Indeed, it may be their virtue which unsticks them. And then they cannot be said to be happy. But though virtue might bring unhappiness, it was in Aristotle's view a source of fulfilment in itself. Think, for example, of how being physically healthy might somehow get you into trouble. It might leave you with such a ripplingly muscular physique that puny bar-flies can't resist taking an envious smack at you. But being healthy remains enjoyable in itself. Aristotle also thought that if you did not act well, you were punished not by hell fire or a sudden bolt from heaven, but by having to live a damaged, crippled life.

You cannot, of course, believe all this and be an anti-essentialist as well. Anti-essentialists do not believe in natures in the first place. They imagine that for something to have a nature means that it must be eternally fixed and unalterable. In their view, talk of nature also brings out what is common to certain things, an unpopular thing to do in an age which makes a supreme value of difference. Critics of essentialism also suspect with some justice that, when it comes to human beings rather than giraffes, the answer 'It's just in my nature' is usually a shifty self-rationalization. Destroying tribal communities in the pursuit of profit is just part of human nature. Being a wife-beater is simply what I am. Anti-essentialists are therefore wary of the idea of nature, just as the apologists of capitalism are. Capitalism wants men and women to be infinitely pliable and adaptable. As a system, it has a Faustian horror of fixed boundaries, of anything which offers an obstacle to the infinite accumulation of capital. If it is a thoroughly materialist system in one sense, it is a virulently anti-material one in another. Materiality is what gets in its way. It is the inert, recalcitrant stuff which puts up resistance to its grandiose schemes. Everything solid must be dissolved into air.

The conflict between a traditional belief in human nature and a 'progressive' rejection of it breaks out between Macbeth and Lady Macbeth, just before they set about killing the king:

MACBETH:
I dare do all that may become a man;
Who dares do more is none.
LADY MACBETH:
. . . When you durst do it, then you were a man;
And to be more than what you were, you would
Be so much more the man.

(Act 1, scene 7)

It is a quarrel between those like Macbeth who see the constraints of human nature as creative ones, and those like Lady Macbeth for whom being human is a matter of perpetually going beyond them. For Macbeth himself, to overreach those creative constraints is to undo yourself, becoming nothing in the act of seeking to be all. It is what the ancient Greeks knew as hubris. For Lady Macbeth, there is no such constraining nature: humanity is free to invent and reinvent itself at will, in a potentially endless process. The more you do, the more you are. For his part,

Aristotle would have sided with Macbeth. He thought that the idea of economic production for profit was unnatural, since it involved a boundlessness which is alien to us. The economic, for Aristotle as for socialism, had to be embedded within the moral. Once this unnatural economic system known as capitalism was up and running, however, it was socialism which came in time to seem contrary to human nature.

No way of life in history has been more in love with transgression and transformation, more enamoured of the hybrid and pluralistic, than capitalism. In its ruthlessly instrumental logic, it has no time for the idea of nature – for that whose whole existence consists simply in fulfilling and unfolding itself, purely for its own sake and without any thought of a goal. This is one reason why this social order has a boorish horror of art, which can be seen as the very image of such gloriously pointless fulfilment. It is also one reason why aesthetics has played such a surprisingly important moral and political role in the modern age.

There is no need to imagine, as many anti-essentialists do, that natures need be eternally fixed. The most dramatic example we have of a nature which is perpetually re-making itself is human nature. The champions of transgression are right at least to this extent, that it is in our nature to go beyond ourselves. Because we are the kind of labouring, linguistic, sexual, sociable animals we are, it is in our nature to give birth to culture, which is always changeable, diverse and open-ended. So it is easy to mistake the peculiar kind of nature we have for no nature at all, and come like the champions of transgression to cultivate a Faustian image of ourselves. We can fantasize, as so much so-called 'materialist' cultural theory does, that culture takes over from our material nature entirely, eradicates every last trace of it, and so can dance on its grave.

Another reason why it is easy to think this way is because the concept of nature is often linked to the idea of function. When a watch is fulfilling its function of telling the time accurately, it is a good watch, doing the kind of thing that watches ought to do. At the risk of sounding mildly ridiculous, we can speak of it as fulfilling its nature. But what is the function of human beings? What are human beings *for*? The answer is surely: nothing – but this, precisely, is the point. Our function is to be functionless. It is to realize our nature as an end in itself. We need the word 'nature' here to avoid having to say 'realize *ourselves* as an end in itself', since a good deal of what we are capable of should by no means see the light of day. So 'nature' here means something like 'the way we are most likely to flourish'. And since what this involves is by no means obvious, this is another reason why it is easy to mistake this situation for not having a nature at all.

This is the mistake of the anti-essentialists. They might concede that humans have a nature in a physical, material sense – that there are certain peculiar features which characterize us as a species. (Though there is no need to assume that there is therefore a sharp break between humans and other animals, Nature abhorring sharp breaks as much as it does vacuums.) It is just that they see no particular moral or political consequences as following from this. For them, it is too general a way of talking to tell us anything very informative. It is true enough, but vacuous. The anti-essentialists are right to complain that talk of human nature is disturbingly general. But one danger for them is falling into a form of idealism. If you play down the material 'species being' of humanity, you may be left assuming that human beings exist only at the level of meaning and value. And this is a convenient mistake for intellectuals to make.

The political philosopher John O'Neill has pointed out that most of what postmodern thinkers criticize as 'essentialist' is a caricature of the doctrine of essences which is defended by nobody.[3] Essentialism, he points out, is the belief that there are properties which some things need to have if they are to be the kind of things they are. For something to be copper, it must have ductility, malleability, fusibility, electricial conductivity, atom number 29, and so on. It does not follow that all the properties of an object are essential to it, or that there cannot be a great deal of difference and diversity between objects of the same class. All sheep are unique. Essentialism does not mean uniformity. Neither does it follow that all the objects assigned to the same class actually do share essential properties in common. We have to look and see. Essentialism does not involve ignoring the difference between natural and cultural phenomena. Cultural phenomena can have certain properties without which they would be something else. If songs don't have sounds they are not songs. Anti-essentialism is largely the product of philosophical amateurism and ignorance.

Talk about human nature is indeed embarrassingly general. (Though Aristotle, who subscribed to the idea himself, did not believe that ethics was a matter of universal principles.) 'Human' can be a term of approval ('Despite being the world's leading authority on ectoplasm, he seemed surprisingly human'), or a pejorative judgement, as in 'all too human'. Even if we go a bit further and speak of the good life as one in which you can fulfil your nature as freely and fully as possible, it is still not clear what this means in concrete terms. Human beings have many different powers and capacities at any given historical time, and it is not obvious which of these they should strive to realize, or in which ways. Are we to fulfil our capacity to strangle others,

3. See John O'Neill, *The Market: Ethics, Knowledge and Politics*, London, 1998, ch. 1. See also Terry Eagleton, *The Illusions of Postmodernism*, Oxford, 1996, pp. 97–104.

simply because we are physically able to do so? If we are able to torture others, then there is a sense in which torture is natural to us. 'Human nature' can describe the kind of creatures we are, or it can mean how we *should* behave; and it is not easy to see how we can leap from the descriptive sense to the normative one.

Aristotle thought that there was a particular way of living which allowed us, so to speak, to be at our best for the kind of creatures we are. This was the life conducted according to the virtues. The Judaeo-Christian tradition considers that it is the life of charity or love. What this means, roughly speaking, is that we become the occasion for each other's self-realization. It is only through being the means of your self-fulfilment that I can attain my own, and vice versa. There is little about such reciprocity in Aristotle himself. The political form of this ethic is known as socialism, for which, as Marx comments, the free development of each is the condition for the free development of all. It is, as it were, politicized love, or reciprocity all round.

Socialism is an answer to the question of what happens when, unlike Aristotle, we universalize the idea of self-realization, crossing it with the Judaeo-Christian or democratic-Enlightenment creed that everyone must be in on the action. If this is so, and if human beings naturally live in political society, we can either try to arrange political life so that they all realize their unique capacities without getting in each other's way, a doctrine known as liberalism; or we can try to organize political institutions so that their self-realization is as far as possible reciprocal, a theory known as socialism. One reason for judging socialism to be superior to liberalism is the belief that human beings are political animals not only in the sense that they have to take account of each other's need for fulfilment, but that in fact they achieve their deepest fulfilment only in terms of each other.

Not everyone, however, agrees on what love or self-fulfilment is, or on which virtues are important, or indeed on this model of the good life at all. The virtues which Aristotle favours are not necessarily the ones which we moderns would be keen to affirm. They are too bound up with his own social history, whereas, conversely, his view of human nature in general is too little historical. Yet Karl Marx, a closet Aristotelian of sorts, conjured a powerfully historical critique from this ethic, as did his great mentor Hegel. It looks as though we simply have to argue with each other about what self-realization means; and it may be that the whole business is too complicated for us to arrive at a satisfactory solution. Modern existence, being fragmentary, specialized and diverse, has come up with too many solutions to the question to make a decision between them at all simple.

Yet there is another reason why the modern period in particular has made moral questions hard to handle. It is not only because in a complex society there are too many answers rather than too few; it is also because modern history makes it especially hard for us to think in non-instrumental terms. Modern capitalist societies are so preoccupied with thinking in terms of means and ends, of which methods will efficiently achieve which goals, that their moral thinking becomes infected by this model as well. What it is to live well thus becomes a matter of acting so as to attain a certain goal. The only problem is that moralists continue to bicker about what the goal should be. For utilitarians, we should act so as to bring about the greatest happiness of the greatest number. For hedonists, we should act so as to maximize pleasure, preferably our own. There have been those who held that the aim of human action was to glorify the political state. Still others believe that we should act so as to achieve social justice or some other praiseworthy end. In a moral climate where what matters seems to be results, some people might well think twice about trying to help an injured man if they knew that the roof was about to fall in on him and finish him off. Yet a lot of people would help him all the same, and it is interesting to ask ourselves why.

Not all modern moral thinking is of this instrumental kind. In fact, one of the most influential schools of modern moral thought – the one deriving from the philosopher Immanuel Kant – is of just the opposite persuasion. For Kantians, what matters is not goals, but the purity of will with which we act in a certain way regardless of its consequences, and regardless of its contribution to our happiness. Morality is a question of duty, not of pleasure, fulfilment, utility or social justice. We might see this austere, unworldly moral doctrine as being, among other things, an overreaction to goal-oriented thinking. It is as though such goals as happiness, pleasure and the like have become so brittle and banal in modern society that authentic moral value must now be rigorously severed from them. Kant is right that to act morally should be an end in itself. It is not just a matter of trying to get somewhere. But he can only formulate this in a way which divorces end-in-itselfness from happiness and fulfilment. And it is precisely this combination that a more classical kind of moral thought is trying to get at.

For classical moralists like Aristotle, happiness or well-being consists not just in bovine contentment or a state of perpetual orgasmic pleasure, but in a life which one might describe as thriving or flourishing. The word 'flourishing' may carry rather virile, strenuous, red-faced connotations for us, but it need not do so. It includes, say, showing mercy or sympathetic listening. We need to take the idea of flourishing out of the gym. We live well when we fulfil our nature as an enjoyable end in itself. And since our nature is something we share with other creatures of our kind, morality is an inherently political matter. As Philippa Foot remarks, 'to know whether an individual is or is not as it should be, one must know the life form of the species'.[4]

The good life, then, is all about an enjoyable well-being, but that is not its immediate aim. Making enjoyment the end of your life, as, say, Mick Jagger seems remarkably successful at doing, may mean that you have to devote a lot of time to planning for it, which in turn may have the result of making your life less enjoyable. This does not seem to be the most tragic deficiency in Mick Jagger's life, but it makes the point that if you really want self-fulfilment, the best way is not to think about yourself. This is not to commend the altruism of the downtrodden, who forget about their own needs so as to keep someone else in clover. It is just to say that well-being is not something you aim at directly, since it is not one good among others. Rather, it is the result of many different kinds of goods. In this sense, Aristotle is a pluralist when it comes to what counts as the good life.

Enjoyment comes from the deep sense of well-being which for Aristotle springs in its turn from living a life of virtue. 'Virtue' here means something like the technique or know-how of being human. Being human is something you have to get good at, like playing snooker or avoiding the rent collector. The virtuous are those who are successful at being human, as a butcher or jazz pianist are successful at their jobs. Some human beings are even virtuosi of virtue. Virtue in this sense is a worldly affair; but it is unworldly in the sense that success is its own reward. Not many company directors would relinquish their salaries on the grounds that their work was a pleasure in itself. The good life is a taxing, technical business; it does not flow from attending to the promptings of the heart. Like a good stage play, it requires a good deal of rehearsal. How to fulfil one's nature doesn't come

4. Philippa Foot, *Natural Goodness*, Oxford, 2001, p. 91.

naturally. But whereas the puritan might well agree with that, he would not agree so easily that the good life is a matter of joyful self-fulfilment. In his view, if it isn't unpleasant, it can't be moral.

This is not to suggest that instrumental ideas of morality should simply be ditched. If we are historical animals, we are bound to be instrumental ones, too, concerned with fitting means to ends. If the good life is one of fulfilling our natures, and if this is true for everybody, then it would take a deep-seated change of material conditions to make such fulfilment possible all round. And this would require the kind of instrumental action known as radical politics. A lot of functional activity would be needed to achieve a situation in which we did not have to live so functionally. In the modern age, this project has been known as socialism.

There is a potentially tragic conflict here between the means and the end. If we have to act instrumentally in order to create a less means-ends-obsessed form of life, then we have to live in a way which by our own admission is less than desirable. At the worst, it may mean that some people, tragically, may feel the need to sacrifice their own happiness for others. To call this tragic means that such sacrifice is not the most desirable way to live. Morality is about fulfilling the self, not abnegating it. It is just that for some people, abnegating it may be historically necessary for bringing that desirable form of life about. There are, tragically, situations in which the self can be fulfilled only by being relinquished. If history were not as dire as it has been, this would not be necessary. In a just world, our condition would not need to be broken in order to be re-made.

What does all this have to do with objectivity? It is that flourishing cannot really be a subjective affair. This does not mean that it is objective in the sense that it has nothing to do with us, rather as the Giant's Causeway is there independently of whether we are there to look at it. Ethics is all about human beings – but it is about what they are like, not what they like. Some kinds of happiness may be subjective, in the sense that people are often contented if they think they are. Sometimes you just have to take their word for it. You may be wrong about think-ing you are happy in some deeper sense of the word, but it is hard to see how you can be wrong about feeling gratified and at ease, any more than you can have a pain and not know about it.

The kind of happiness that matters, however, is the kind which is much less easy to determine. You cannot tell whether your life is flourishing simply by introspection, because it is a matter of how you are doing, not just of how you are feeling. Happiness is about living and acting well, not just about feeling good. For Aristotle, it is a practice or activity rather than a state of mind. It is about realizing your capacities, not having a particular outlook on life.

Rather than simply checking out how you are feeling, you have to look at your life in a much wider context. It is this wider context which Aristotle knows as politics. You also have to look at yourself in a temporal context – to have some sense of your life as a narrative, in order to judge whether it is going well or not. This does not mean that everything from cutting your first teeth to losing the lot of them has to form a logically coherent whole. Not many narratives of any degree of subtlety have that kind of unity. Narratives can be multiple, ruptured, recursive and diffuse and still be narratives. Finally, you have to have some idea of what counts as a specifically human kind of prospering. It is not just an individual affair. It is not up to you to decide what counts as this, any more than it is up to you to decide what counts as mental stability in a moose. You cannot say 'Torturing Tyroleans feels like thriving for *me*' – not just because it is not true, but because it is not up to you to lay down the law. Moral values are not just what you happen to plump for, as the decisionist or existentialist maintains. Some moral thinkers believe that they are what all of us happen to plump for – that they are intersubjective rather than subjective. But this way of looking at morality does not. Even if we were all to agree that torturing Tyroleans was an excellent idea, it would still not count as an instance of human flourishing. Some people would consider this an impossibly objectivist position, though probably not Tyroleans.

Another reason why you cannot know whether you are flourishing just by looking inside yourself is because the idea of flourishing is a complex one, involving a whole range of factors. You may be prospering in some ways and not in others. You have to ask yourself whether you are healthy, happy, at ease with yourself and others, enjoying life, working creatively, emotionally caring and sensitive, resilient, capable of fulfilling friendships, responsible, self-reliant and the like. A lot of these things are not wholly within your control. You cannot be happy or at ease with yourself just by an act of will. It requires among other things certain social and material conditions.

Whether you can live a moral life, which is to say a fulfilling life of a kind proper to human beings, depends in the end on politics. This is one reason why Aristotle makes no rigorous distinction between ethics and politics. He tells us right at the beginning of his *Nicomachean Ethics* that there is a 'science that studies the supreme good for man', adding rather unexpectedly that it is known as politics. Ethics for him is a sort of sub-branch of politics. Nobody can thrive when they are starving, miserable or oppressed, a fact which did not prevent Aristotle himself from endorsing slavery and the subordination of women. If you want to be good, you need a good society. Of course there can be saints in atrocious social conditions, but part of what we admire about such people is their rarity. Basing an ethics on this would be like restricting everyone to three raw carrots a day simply because a few rather weird people can survive happily on such a diet.

Ethics is in Aristotle's view the science of human desire, since desire is the motive behind all our actions. The task of an ethical education is to re-educate our desires, so that we reap pleasure from doing good acts and pain from doing bad ones. It is not just a matter of gritting our teeth and capitulating to some imperious moral law: we need to learn to enjoy being just, merciful, independent and so on. If there is not something in it for us, it is not true morality. And since all our desires are social, they have to be set in a wider context, which is politics. Radical politics is the re-education of our desires. Aristotle was not of course a radical, but he held that playing an active part in political life was itself a virtuous thing to do. Republicanism is an ethical form of politics. Being politically active helps us to create the social conditions for virtue, but it is also a form of virtue in itself. It is both a means and an end.

You can, then, be mistaken about whether you are flourishing, and someone else may be more wisely perceptive about the matter than you yourself. This is one important sense in which morality is objective. Feeling happy may be a sign that you are thriving as a human being should, whatever that means; but it is not cast-iron evidence. You might be feeling happy because the parents of your abductee have just come up with the ransom money. Or it might be a rare patch of felicity in a generally dispirited existence. The point, anyway, is that when the colonialists assure us that the natives are thriving, we would do well to be cautious.

The problems arise when the natives themselves tell us that they are thriving. What are we to say then? The liberal or postmodernist who is reluctant to say that the colonialists are right may also hesitate to say that the people they lord it over are wrong. Have we not patronized the colonized enough without informing them that they are too thick-headed to realize they are miserable? In fact, it is deeply unlikely that men and women who are treated as second-class human beings would be obtuse enough to believe that they were prospering. If they lacked that kind of intelligence, they would probably not be usefully exploitable in the first place. They might feel gratified now and then, or believe that they deserve nothing better, or be stoical about their situation, but that is different. Anyway, if I cannot tell you something without odious patronage, neither can you tell me. Even though I have been buried under a ton of rotting asbestos for the last ten years, with only three fingers free to cram the odd forkful of withered grass into my craw, I will not stand being told by condescending elitists like you that there might be a better way to live. My decisions may be abysmal, but at least they are mine.

There are, then, certain public criteria to determine whether we, or somebody else, are flourishing or not. I cannot see that I am doing well just by looking into my soul. As Ludwig Wittgenstein remarked, the best image of the soul is the human body. The best image of what I am is how I am behaving. The two are as closely bound up with each other as a word and its meaning. These public criteria provide us with a case against those for whom happiness or well-being is not a practical condition but an individual state of mind. But happiness is not just a state of mind, any more than playing chess is just a state of mind. People may feel content with their situation; but if they are not, for example, allowed to play an active role in determining their own lives, then in Aristotle's eyes they cannot be genuinely fulfilled. Virtue for Aristotle is a kind of excellence; and though slaves may feel in good shape from time to time, they are not exactly object-lessons in how to excel at being human. If they were, we would not bother to free them. Objectivity is among other things a political affair: it is a matter of there being ways of refuting those who insist that all is well as long as we are feeling fine. It is a critique of the holiday-camp mentality. Or, as Bertolt Brecht put it rather less politely, 'the scum who want the cockles of their hearts warmed'. To feel good about yourself when you have no material grounds for doing so is to do yourself an injustice.

There is, however, an even deeper relation between objectivity and ethics. Objectivity can mean a selfless openness to the needs of others, one which lies very close to love. It is the opposite not of personal interests and convictions, but of egoism. To try to see the other's situation as it really is is an essential condition of caring for them. This is not to say that there is only ever one way a situation can be said to be. To say that 'writing a book' is an accurate description of what I am doing right now is not to say that it is the only way it can be described. The point, anyway, is that genuinely caring for someone is not what gets in the way of seeing their situation for what it is, but what makes it possible. Contrary to the adage that love is blind, it is because love involves a radical acceptance that it allows us to see others for what they are.

To be concerned for another is to be present to them in the form of an absence, a certain self-forgetful attentiveness. If one is loved or trusted in return, it is largely this which gives one the self-confidence to forget about oneself, a perilous matter otherwise. We need to think about ourselves partly because of fear, which the assurance which flows from being trusted allows us to overcome. To achieve such objectivity in any absolute way we would need to remove ourselves from the situation altogether, which would hardly be the most convenient way of intervening in it. But the fact that it is ultimately impossible should not deter us from trying to achieve it.

Trying to be objective is an arduous, fatiguing business, which in the end only the virtuous can attain. Only those with patience, honesty, courage and persistence can delve through the dense layers of self-deception which prevent us from seeing the situation as it really is. This is especially difficult for those who wield power – for power tends to breed fantasy, reducing the self to a state of querulous narcissism. For all its tough-minded pragmatism, it is riddled with delusion, assuming that the whole world centres subserviently upon itself. It dissolves reality to a mirror of its own desires. It is those whose material existence is pretty solid who tend to assume that the world is not. Power is naturally solipsistic, incapable of getting outside its own skin. Like sexuality, it is where we are most infantile. It is the powerless who are more likely to appreciate that the world does not exist to pander to our needs, and rolls on its own sweet way with scarcely a side-glance at us.

Knowledge and morality, then, are not finally separable, as the modern age has tended to assume. One can see this particularly in the case of our knowledge of each other, which involves moral capacities like imagination, sensitivity, emotional intelligence and the like. Knowing another person is not like knowing the flashiest bars in Rio; it is kind of knowledge bound up with moral value. The modern age drives a wedge between knowledge and morality, fact and value; but since establishing the facts is usually a gruelling process, given the complexity of the world, the deceptiveness of some of its appearances, and our own chronic tendency to self-delusion, it is bound to involve value of a kind. Knowledge needs to be disciplined, judicious, meticulous, self-critical, discriminating and so on, so that nobody without some sort of virtue could write a great history of the boll weevil or come up with a stunning scientific discovery. Perhaps this was what Ludwig Wittgenstein had in mind when he asked himself how he could be a good logician without being a decent human being. Nobody who was not open to dialogue with others, willing to listen, argue honestly and admit when he or she was wrong could make real headway in investigating the world.

To see the other's situation as it really is is the opposite of sentimentalism. Sentimentalism sees the world as benignly coloured by itself, whereas selfishness colours the world malignly with itself. The opposite of this self-centredness, for which the world is just an imaginary doubling of one's ego, is what modern theory calls 'decentring', or what has been more traditionally known as disinterestedness. Disinterestedness, a notion almost universally scorned by the cultural left nowadays for its bogus impartiality, grew up in the eighteenth century as the opposite not of interests, but of self-interest. It was a weapon to wield against the Hobbesians and possessive individualists. Disinterestedness means not viewing the world from some sublime Olympian height, but a kind of compassion or fellow-feeling. It means trying to feel your way imaginatively into the experience of another, sharing their delight and sorrow without thinking of oneself.[5] George Eliot is one of the great nineteenth-century inheritors of this ethical lineage. To this extent, the moral and the aesthetic are closely allied. It is not that we do not have interests: it is just that our interest lies in another rather than in ourselves. This kind of imaginative sympathy, like virtue

5. This, for example, is the notion of disinterestedness of the great eighteenth-century Irish philosopher Francis Hutcheson. See R. S. Downie (ed.), *Francis Hutcheson: Philosophical Writings*, London, 1994.

for Aristotle, is its own reward; it does not seek for profit, but takes pleasure in the well-being of others with a well-nigh sensuous relish. Disinterestedness – for postmodern theory, the last word in delusion – is a smack at the egoistic individualism of early middle-class society. It is in origin a radical political concept.

Striving for dispassionate judgement is an emotionally taxing affair. It does not come at all naturally. Objectivity requires a fair degree of passion – in particular, the passion for doing the kind of justice which might throw open your most deep-seated prejudices to revision. Disinterestedness does not mean being magically absolved from interests, but recognizing that some of your interests are doing you no good, or that it is in the interests of doing an effective job to set certain of them apart for the moment. It demands imagination, sympathy and self-discipline. You do not need to rise majestically above the fray to decide that in a specific situation, somebody else's interests should be promoted over yours. On the contrary, to judge this accurately involves being in the thick of the affray, assessing the situation from the inside, not loitering in some no man's land where you would be incapable of knowing anything. You do not have to be standing in metaphysical outer space to recognize that sending your valet off on a fifteen-mile walk through bandit-infested woods in the dead of winter to buy you a small bar of Turkish Delight should yield precedence to letting him linger by his father's deathbed. Someone who insisted on dispatching the valet would be being unreasonable – a point worth pondering for those for whom it is reason, not unreason, which is cold and clinical.

Of course you may spare the valet his fifteen-mile hike for self-interested reasons. Perhaps you want to overwhelm him with your generosity so as to get away with slashing his wages, or fear that he may deliberately burn your underwear in an act of reprisal when he next irons it. What counts, however, is what you do. It is not that your intentions do not matter at all, just that they matter less. An obsession with intentions has been the bugbear of some moral thought. It is thus a point in favour of the classical ethics we have been examining that for it, moral value lies in the world rather than in your mind. In that sense, it resembles meaning, which is in the first place in history rather than our heads.

Virtue for Aristotle is not a state of mind but a disposition – which means being permanently geared for acting in a certain way even when you are not acting at all. It is a matter of how you would customarily behave in a given situation. Goodness is a matter of habit. Like playing the flute, you get better at it the more you practise. It is not, as we post-Romantics tend to assume, that we start off with inner moral feelings which then issue in actions. This would be like imagining that someone could spend three years learning inwardly how to play the flute, pick up the instrument and coax it instantly into melodious sound. It is rather that our actions create the appropriate states of mind. We become brave or generous by habitually doing brave or generous things. This, once more, is rather like the question of meaning. We do not have the concept of exasperation and then put it into words; having the concept of exasperation is a matter of being familiar with the social custom of how the word is used.

Objectivity does not mean judging from nowhere. On the contrary, you can only know how the situation is if you are in a *position* to know. Only by standing at a certain angle to reality can it be illuminated for you. The wretched of the earth, for example, are likely to appreciate more of the truth of human history than their masters – not because they are innately more perceptive, but because they can glean from their own everyday experience that history for the vast majority of men and women has been largely a matter of despotic power and fruitless toil. As Michael Hardt and Antonio Negri put the point in their study *Empire*: 'Only the poor lives radically the actual and present being, in destitution and suffering, and thus only the poor has the ability to renew being.'[6] Only those who know how calamitous things actually are can be sufficiently free of illusion or vested interests to change them. You cannot change the situation effectively unless you appreciate the depth of the problem; and to do that fully you need to be at the sticky end of it, or at least to have heard the news from there.

At the level of tacit or informal knowledge, then, the poor know better than their governors how it is with history. Objectivity and partisanship are allies, not rivals. What is not conducive to objectivity on this score is the judicious even-handedness of the liberal. It is the liberal who falls for the myth that you can only see things aright if you don't take sides. It is the industrial chaplain view of reality. The liberal has difficulty with situations in which one side has a good deal more of the truth than the other – which is to say, all the key political situations. For this is to equate truth with one-sidedness rather than with symmetry, which is not how liberals tend to see the matter. For them, the truth generally lies somewhere in the middle. Or, as Raymond Williams once commented: when in doubt, the Englishman thinks of a pendulum. Faced with the poor's view of history as for the most part wretchedness and adversity, the liberal reaches instinctively to trim the balance: hasn't there also been a great deal of splendour and value? Indeed there has; but

6. Michael Hardt and Antonio Negri, *Empire*, Cambridge, Mass., 2000, p. 157.

to claim that the two balance each other out is surely to falsify. Even-handedness here is not in the service of objectivity. True judiciousness means taking sides.

We tend to think of the subjective as pertaining to the self, and the objective to the world. The subjective is a matter of value, while the world is a matter of fact. And how these two come together is often something of a mystery. Yet one way in which they converge is in the act of self-reflection. Or, if you like, in that curious somersault or backward flip in which the self takes itself as an object of knowledge. Objectivity is not just a condition outside the self. In the form of self-knowledge, it is the pre-condition of all successful living. Self-knowledge is inseparably a matter of fact and value. It is a question of knowing your self, but this very act of knowing reflects a kind of value which is beyond the reach of orchids and alligators.

If knowing the world often enough means burrowing through complex swathes of self-deception, knowing oneself involves this even more. Only someone unusually secure could have the courage to confront themselves in this way without either rationalizing away what they unearth, or being consumed by fruitless guilt. Only someone confident of being loved and trusted can achieve that kind of security. This is another linkage between knowledge and moral value. Since fear is one of our natural conditions, men and women can only truly make themselves known to those whom they love or trust. As the Duke comments to the cynical Lucio in Shakespeare's *Measure for Measure*, 'Love talks with better knowledge, and knowledge with dearer love.' In the act of trusting self-disclosure, knowledge and value go hand in hand. Similarly, only if one knows that one will still be accepted can one dare to encounter the truth of oneself. In these senses, too, value and objectivity are not the opposites which so many seem to think them.

One of the opposites of objectivity is narcissism. To believe that the world is an object independent of my life is to accept that it will trundle on with supreme indifference after my death.[7] This is at once pure speculation on my part, since I will not be around to confirm it, and, so to speak, a dead certainty. The world is impeccably democratic and even-handed: it has no regard for any of us. It does not depend for its survival on our favourable opinions of it, as a slave might do on his master's. It is only those who fantasize that reality is the kind of thing that *might* have a regard for them, or maybe once did, who behave like jilted lovers. Those who imagine that the world has taken a shine to them, that its existence depends in some sense on their own, will never be able to grow up. It is true, if Freud is to be credited, that we never grow up anyway, and that maturity is a fantasy entertained only by the young. But there are degrees of infantilism. Supermodels and idealist philosophers rank high in the scale.

Such people are also likely to have problems in acknowledging the autonomy of others. One way in which we recognize that the world is objective is by recognizing the presence of others whose behaviour manifests the fact that, at a very basic level, reality is pretty much the same for them as it is for ourselves. Or, if it seems not to be, then at least there is someone out there with whom we can argue the toss. Indeed, it is others who are the paradigm case of objectivity. They are not only pieces of the world which are independent of us, but the only fragments of the world's furniture which can actually impress upon us this truth. Other persons are objectivity in action. It is exactly because

7. Independence and objectivity, to be sure, are not quite the same thing. But it is because we recognize something as independent of us that the issue of trying to see it as it really is arises. We would not strive to see our hallucinations as they really are.

they are fellow subjects that they can reveal to us their otherness, and in that act disclose to us our own. For conservatives, there is that in the world which cannot be tampered with, known as property. For radicals, too, there is that which is beyond our meddling, known as the autonomy of others. It is this which grounds our notions of objectivity. Liberals, characteristically, back both horses, believing in both property and autonomy.

6

Morality

For a long time, cultural theorists avoided the question of morality as something of an embarrassment. It seemed preachy, unhistorical, priggish and heavy-handed. For the harder-nosed kind of theorist, it was also soppy and unscientific. It was too often just a fancy name for oppressing other people. Morality is a question of what our parents believe, not what we think. Most of it seems to be about sex, or more precisely about why you should not have it. Since having sex in the 1960s was a kind of sacred obligation, like wearing mascara or worshipping your ancestors, morality rapidly gave way to style. Or, indeed, to politics. The ethical was for suburbanites, while the political was cool.

Ethics were for those who made a fuss about whether to go to bed with each other, not for political types. It was not that political types did not go to bed with each other, just that they did not make a fuss about it. So-called moral questions, such as whether to steal an expensive volume of Nietzsche from the local bookstore, could be resolved by asking how far this action was likely to promote or retard the emancipation of the working class. Since it was unlikely to retard that emancipation in any dramatic way, it was probably all right to go ahead and steal it. Whole shelfloads of Nietzsche and Marcuse accordingly disappeared from libraries and bookshops, leaving Walter Scott and the correspondence of Winston Churchill behind.

We have suggested already that this view of morality is a mistaken one. Morality is all about enjoyment and abundance of life, and for classical thought ethics and politics are hard to distinguish. Despite this, cultural theorists felt uneasy with moral questions because they seemed to pass over the political for the personal. Wasn't morality about such matters as keeping your promises and not fornicating, rather than wage agreements and TV franchises? It is true that morality has been often enough a way of ducking hard political questions by reducing them to the personal. In the so-called war against terrorism, for example, the word 'evil' really means: Don't look for a political explanation. It is a wonderfully time-saving device. If terrorists are simply Satanic, then you do not need to investigate what lies behind their atrocious acts of violence. You can ignore the plight of the Palestinian people, or of those Arabs who have suffered under squalid right-wing autocracies supported by the West for its own selfish, oil-hungry purposes.

The word 'evil' transfers the question from this mundane realm to a sinisterly metaphysical one. You cannot acknowledge that the terrible crimes which terrorists commit have a purpose behind them, since to ascribe purposes to such people is to recognize them as rational creatures, however desperately wrong-headed. It is easier to caricature your enemy as a bunch of blood-crazed beasts – a deeply dangerous move, since to defeat an opponent you have first to understand him. The British tabloid press may have seen the IRA as gorillas rather than guerrillas, savages with no rationale for their actions, but British Intelligence knew better. They understood that Republican murders and massacres were not without a purpose. Indeed, to label your enemy as mad is to let him, morally speaking, off the hook, absolving him of responsibility for his crimes.

To define morality in purely individual terms is to believe, say, that a history of abuse and emotional deprivation has nothing whatsoever to do with a teenager becoming a petty criminal. It is sometimes pointed out by those who hold this view that not all abused children become criminals; but then not all smokers develop lung cancer. This does not refute the relation between the two. Moral values must be as independent of social forces as artistic ones. The fear lurking behind this view is that to explain is to condone – that one will fall for a sentimentalist, social-worker theory of morality which disavows the reality of human wickedness.

Yet almost nobody believes that to explain the complex historical factors involved in the rise of Hitler is to forgive him his crimes. At least almost nobody believes that now, though at the time it might well have been seen as a thought crime. It is partly because terrorism is here and now that political explanations are considered to lend it comfort, even though political explanations will in fact help to defeat it. On a more moderate version of this view, there are certain immoral acts which we can explain in social terms, and a special class of acts known as evil which we cannot. We shall be taking issue with this opinion later on.

Appeals to morality, like appeals to psychology, have often enough been a way of avoiding political argument. Protestors don't have a point, they just had over-indulgent parents. Women who object to Cruise missiles are simply consumed by penis-envy. Anarchists are the effect of poor potty training. In the light of classical moral thought, all this is deeply ironic. For Aristotle, as we have seen, ethics and politics are intimately related. Ethics is about excelling at being human, and nobody can do this in isolation. Moreover, nobody can do it unless the political institutions which allow you to do it are available. It is this kind of moral thinking which was inherited by Karl Marx, who was much indebted to Aristotle even in his economic thought. Questions of good and bad had been falsely abstracted from their social contexts, and had to be restored to them again. In this sense, Marx was a moralist in the classical sense of the word. He believed that moral inquiry had to examine all of the factors which went to make up a specific action or way of life, not just personal ones.

Unfortunately, Marx was a classical moralist who did not seem aware that he was, rather as Dante was not aware that he was living in the middle ages. Like a lot of radicals since his time, Marx thought on the whole that morality was just ideology.[1] This is because he made the characteristically bourgeois mistake of confusing morality with moralism. Moralism believes that there is a set of questions known as moral questions which are quite distinct from social or political ones. It does not see that 'moral' means exploring the texture and quality of human behaviour as richly and sensitively as you can, and that you cannot do this by abstracting men and women from their social surroundings. This is morality as, say, the novelist Henry James understood it, as opposed to those who believe you can reduce it to rules, prohibitions and obligations.

1. Typical of this view are these words of Fredric Jameson's, one of several such formulations in his work: '. . . ethics, wherever it makes its reappearance, may be taken as the sign of an intent to mystify, and in particular to replace the complex and ambivalent judgements of a more properly political and dialectical perspective with the comfortable simplifications of a binary myth' (*Fables of Aggression*, Berkeley and Los Angeles, 1979, p. 56). Not only is Jameson mistaken to believe that all ethics displaces politics; he also assumes inaccurately that ethics is always a rigid binary matter of good versus evil. It is an oversimplifying account of a supposedly oversimplifying phenomenon.

Marx, however, made the mistake of defining morality as moralism, and so quite understandably rejected it. He did not seem to realize that he was the Aristotle of the modern age. The paradigm of classical morality in our own time has been feminism, which insists in its own way on the interwovenness of the moral and political, power and the personal. It is in this tradition above all that the precious heritage of Aristotle and Marx has been deepened and renewed. This is not to imagine that the personal and the political are the same thing. One can overpoliticize as well as overpersonalize. The English feminist who in a moment of irascibility once considered wearing a lapel-badge reading 'The personal is personal too, so sod off' was making precisely this point. It is just that the distinction between the personal and the political is not the same as that between the moral and the political. And it is feminism, above all, which has been the custodian of this precious insight in our time.

To grasp morality as a great novelist understands it is to see it as an intricately woven texture of nuances, qualities and fine gradations. Novels convey moral truths, though not in any sense of the term that Oral Roberts or Ian Paisley would recognize. A novel with a moral is not likely to be morally interesting. 'Goldilocks' is not the most profound of fables. But this, as we have seen, is not to dismiss rules, principles and obligations out of hand. Indeed, there are quite a few of them in Henry James. It is rather to set them in a different context. Some ways of behaving are so vital to the flourishing of human life all round, or alternatively so injurious to it, that we hedge them around with laws, principles and obligations. They are part of the scaffolding of the good life, not ends in themselves. It is not that principles are unbending while the rest of our conduct is a matter of rule-of-thumb. Principles can be flexible and still be principles. It is not their unbendability which distinguishes them from the rest of our life. It is the vital nature of what they safeguard or promote – vital from the viewpoint of fostering an abundance of life. You can't do this, for example, unless you have a law prohibiting unjust killing. Any thriving form of life will have its obligations and prohibitions. The only problem is that you may then come to identify morality with the obligations and prohibitions, rather than with the thriving.

This is roughly St Paul's position on the Mosaic Law. St Paul is critical of the law, but not because he makes the mistake of assuming that the law of Judaism is just about ritual observances and legalistic prohibitions, whereas the Christian gospel is about love. As a devout Jew himself, St Paul understands perfectly well that the Mosaic law *is* the law of love and justice. It is not just a neurotic fussing about washing and diet. It was not contrary to Jewish law to set the law aside in the name of human compassion. The law against fashioning graven images of God, for example, is really a prohibition on fetishism. To carve a totem of God is to make an ideological idol of him, which you can then manipulate as a magical device to get him to fall in with your wishes. For the Jewish scriptures, you cannot manufacture images of God or even give him a name, because the only image of God is humanity. And humanity is equally resistant to definition. Another such ideological fetish is labour, which is why the law insists that men and women are granted a periodic rest from it on the sabbath. It has nothing to do with going to church. There were no churches. It has to do with leisure.

Similarly, the prohibition on stealing has almost certainly nothing to do with private property. Most Old Testament scholars would now agree that it was probably about stealing people: kidnapping. Quite a lot of this went on at the time, not least so you could lay your hands on the labour-power of young men from other tribes. The Old Testament Jews were not so flush in private property that they needed a special edict from Mount Sinai on the subject – as opposed, say, to adultery, which was rather more in evidence. Honouring your father and your mother is almost certainly about how to treat the old and economically useless of the tribe, not about the nuclear family. There was no nuclear family.

The idea that the Old Testament Jews were a bunch of bureaucratic legalists is a piece of Christian anti-Semitism. It is already present in the sporadically anti-Semitic New Testament, which caricatures the Pharisees in this manner. The Pharisees were certainly purists, but they were also anti-imperial Jewish nationalists sympathetic to the revolutionary underground Zealots. Quite a lot of what Jesus has to say sounds like standard Pharisaical stuff – though he cursed the Pharisees pretty ferociously as well, partly perhaps to put some daylight between them and himself.

Equally, there can be no love without law. Love for the Judaeo-Christian tradition means acting in certain material ways, not feeling a warm glow in your heart. It means, say, caring for the sick and imprisoned, not feeling Romantic about them. And all this occasionally needs to be codified, partly because the poor need the law for their protection. They would be foolish to rely on the big-hearted whimsicality of their superiors. Love is a notoriously obscure, complicated affair, and moral language is a way of trying to get what counts as love into sharper focus. The injunction to love your neighbour is not a Christian invention, but stems from the Old Testament Book of Leviticus. People did not have to wait upon the arrival of an obscure first-century Jewish prophet, who was probably less of a crowd-puller than his mentor John the Baptist, in order to start being nice to each other.

Laws have to be precise because the result of fuzziness may be injustice. A rapist may get off because a legal draughtsman was too vague. Those negotiating with harsh employers would be well advised to seek a contract as tightly worded as possible. The spirit of the law is not always to be preferred to its letter. If Shakespeare's Shylock sticks 'inhumanly' to the letter of his bond, it is for one reason because in doing so he seeks to expose the hypocrisy of a Christian ruling class which will resort to any shabby stratagem or disingenuous verbal quibbling to get one of their own kind off the hook. Shylock's legalism might show up their own, in a monstrous parody of it. And this, for a contemptible Jew, would be no mean achievement.

The exactitude of the law, then, is not to be deplored in some bout of soft-hearted sentimentalism. Jesus rails against legalism, but for the most part he upholds the Judaic law. One reason why the Jewish ruling class handed him over to the Roman colonial power was perhaps because they could not agree that he had violated the Mosaic Law. The law needs to be ruthlessly impersonal so as to treat all those who take shelter under it in an equal manner. 'Privilege' means 'private law'. Treating people in an equal manner does not mean treating them as if they were all the same; it means attending even-handedly to each individual's unique situation. Equality means giving as much weight to one individual's particularity as to another's. We shall see later that there is a similar kind of inhuman anonymity about love.

It is just that for St Paul, the law is really for children and novices. It is for those who are not yet morally independent, and who therefore have to be propped up by a scaffolding of codes and censures. They have not yet developed the spontaneous habit of virtue, and still see morality in superstitious fashion as a matter of offending or placating some higher authority. They have the toddler's theory of ethics. The law may help them to grow into an enjoyable moral autonomy, but they will have done so only when they are able to throw its crutch away and manage by themselves. In a similar way, we know that someone is fluent in Albanian when they are able to dispense with the dictionary. Or we can see that someone's artistic career has really taken fire when she begins to stretch and improvise on the rules of painting or prosody she has been taught. Learning the rules helps her to intuit when to throw them away.

It was not long before cultural theorists came to realize that you could not live without moral discourse altogether. Those in political power might be capable of this feat, because they could always define their power purely in administrative terms. Politics was the technical business of public administration, whereas morality was a private affair. Politics belonged to the boardroom, and morality to the bedroom. This led to a lot of immoral boardrooms and politically oppressive bedrooms. Because politics had been redefined as purely calculative and pragmatic, it was now almost the opposite of the ethical. But since it was hardly barefaced enough to shuck off the ethical altogether, politics had to be conducted in the name of certain moral values which at the same time it could not avoid violating. Power needed those values to lend itself legitimacy, but they also threatened to get seriously in its way. This is one reason why we could now be witnessing the dawn of a new, post-ethical epoch, in which world powers no longer bother to dress up their naked self-interest in speciously altruistic language, but are insolently candid about it instead.

The political left, however, cannot define the political in this purely technical way, since its brand of emancipatory politics inescapably involves questions of value. The problem for some traditional leftist thought was that the more you tried to firm up your political agenda, making it a scientific, materialist affair rather than an idle utopian dream, the more you threatened to discredit the very values it aimed to realize. It seemed impossible to establish, say, the idea of justice on a scientific basis; so what exactly did you denounce capitalism, slavery or sexism in the name of? You cannot describe someone as oppressed unless you have some dim notion of what not being oppressed might look like, and why being oppressed is a bad idea in the first place. And this involves normative judgements, which then makes politics look uncomfortably like ethics.

On the whole, cultural theory has proved fairly unsuccessful at this business. It has been unable to argue convincingly against those who see nothing wrong with shackling or ill-treating others. The only reason it has got away with this so far is that there are few such people around. Almost everybody agrees that exploiting people is wrong. It is just that they cannot agree on why they agree on this. Neither can they agree on what counts as exploitation, which is why, for example, the socialist critique of capitalism, or the feminist critique of patriarchy, are far from self-evident. To see a situation as abusive or exploitative is inevitably to offer an interpretation of it. We will only see it as such within a certain context of assumptions. Oppression is not there before our eyes in the sense that a patch of purple is.

Does this mean that oppression is just a matter of opinion? Not at all. To argue over whether a situation is anti-Semitic or not is to clash over our interpretations of what is going on, not over our subjective reponses to it. It is not a matter of our both seeing the same set of morally neutral physical actions, to which you then add the subjective value-judgement 'good' and I add the subjective value-judgement 'bad'. Moral language is not just a set of notions we use to record our approval or disapproval of actions; it enters into the description of the actions themselves. If I describe an anti-Semitic assault in purely physiological terms, I am not seeing what actually happened. We cannot describe what is actually there without recourse to the beliefs and motivations which it involves. In the same way, we could not describe to an observer ignorant of children what was happening when one small child snatched a toy from another, without resort to concepts like envy, rivalry and resentment. And this is one sense in which moral language is not just subjective.

The radical has two ways of answering the question of why exploitation is wrong, neither of which seems all that appealing. You can go universal and speak of what belongs to the dignity of humanity as a species; or you can go local, and see ideas of freedom and justice as springing from traditions which, despite being purely cultural and historical, nonetheless exert a compelling force over us. The problem with the first approach is that it seems to squeeze out history, whereas the problem with the second approach is that it seems too narrowly invested in it. The first appears too general to be of much use, while the second runs into the usual problems of moral relativism. What if your tribe or tradition, like Aristotle's, finds nothing wrong with slavery? Does this make it acceptable? Is it all right for you to hold that revenge is immoral, but all right for your colonial subjects not to? Are they simply not up to such high-minded ideals? Is the point to understand the cannibals rather than to change them? If so, why does this not also apply to drug traffickers?

By and large, cultural theory has been massively evasive on these matters, on the rare occasions when it has got round to raising them. But the period when this was more or less acceptable may be coming to an end. At the moment, pragmatic kinds of moral justification are popular in the West. We believe in, say, freedom of speech or the inevitability of a degree of unemployment because that is part of our cultural heritage. It is an entirely contingent heritage, with no metaphysical backing to it; but so by the same logic is your alternative way of doing things. If we can give no absolute force to our values, you can offer no knock-down arguments against them. In a sense, we do what we do because we do what we do. After a long enough while, history becomes its own justification, as Edmund Burke insisted in defending the British Empire and the House of Lords. Custom and practice are the best arguments of all.

This kind of case, associated not only with Romantic conservatives like Burke but with postmodern philosophers like Richard Rorty, has served Western civilization tolerably well in these post-metaphysical times. But its hour, for all that, may be about to strike. For one thing, it becomes harder to justify your form of life in such laid-back, off-the-cuff terms when it has launched upon a new extremist, globally aggressive phase. The United States government is at present in the hands of extremists and semi-fanatical fundamentalists, and not at all because it has been taken over by al-Qaida. For another thing, it becomes harder for intellectuals to justify a form of life which has grown increasingly lax and nonchalant about justifying itself. Not long ago, Western civilization resorted to various solemn-sounding doctrines to legitimate some of its shadier activities: the Will of God, the Destiny of the West, the White Man's Burden. The embarrassment of these ideals was that they clashed somewhat grotesquely with what people were actually up to. A credibility gap opened up between fact and value, which it was hard to paper over. In practice, capitalism is restive with all restrictions; traditionally, however, it has concealed that anarchic impulse beneath its restrictive moral codes.

As Western capitalism embarks upon its post-metaphysical phase, these codes begin to shed their credibility. The very secular, pragmatic climate which capitalism has itself created lends them the hollow, parsonical ring of a sermon on why God permits genocide. High-sounding hypocrisy begins to give way to arrogantly explicit self-interest. Strict moral codes start to loosen up, as the solidly reputable middle classes become increasingly a thing of the past, and as morals and manners begin to reflect a two-dimensional world of drift, cynicism and self-seeking. Moral values which state what you ought to do are impressively idealistic, but too blatantly at odds with your behaviour; moral values which reflect what you actually do are far more plausible, but only at the cost of no longer serving to legitimate your activity.

In any case, as the Western system in its post-Cold War stage found itself less and less constrained by a political adversary, it was able to expand and intensify its activities in ways which made them harder to conceal beneath a cloak of humanitarianism or global altruism. There were also fewer critics to whom it needed to justify itself. At the same time, however, the rise of a metaphysical adversary of the West, in the shape of fundamentalist Islam, means that the West is in the end going to have to do rather better than claiming that a distaste for authoritarianism or fiddling the books of gigantic corporations just happen to be the kind of thing it goes in for. The more predatory and corrupt capitalism grows, the less easily it can mount convincing defences of its way of life; yet in the face of the rising political hostility caused by its expanding ambitions, the more urgently it needs to do so. However, such appeals to fundamental values may become hard to distinguish from the kind of fundamentalism which the West is out to combat. One way in which its enemies may thus prove victorious is by turning it inexorably into a mirror-image of themselves – and this, ironically, in the very act of the West's struggling to oppose them.

When cultural theory finally did get round to tackling ethical questions, it did so, surprisingly, in a Kantian kind of way.

Surprisingly, because Kant's moral thought is absolutist in a way at odds with the drift of much contemporary theory. The austere climate of Kantian ethics hardly consorts well with the hedonistic playfulness of postmodern thought. (It is true, however, that some of that theory has even managed to convert play into a solemn, cerebral, mildly intimidating affair.) The kind of moral theory which began finally to emerge, in the work of critics and philosophers like Paul de Man, Emmanuel Levinas, Jacques Derrida, Jean-François Lyotard and J. Hillis Miller, was that of a mysterious, unknowable moral law, embodied for us in some Other, which laid upon us an absolute, unconditional demand, and which evoked from us an equally infinite sense of responsibility.[2]

On this viewpoint, there are moral judgements, but they lack any sort of criteria or rational basis. There is no longer any relation, as there was for Aristotle or Marx, between the way the world is and how we ought to act within it, or between the way we are and what we ought to do. Because the way we and the world are, for these thinkers, is no way in particular, they cannot serve as a basis for moral judgement. Those judgements are accordingly left hanging in the air, demanded of us in apparently gratuitous fashion by some sublimely enigmatic Law or Other. For Jacques Derrida, ethics is a matter of absolute decisions – decisions which are vital and necessary but also utterly 'impossible', and which fall outside all given norms, forms of knowledge and modes of conceptualization.[3] One can

2. For an account of this version of ethics, see Terry Eagleton, 'Deconstruction and Human Rights', in Barbara Johnson (ed.), *Freedom and Interpretation*, New York, 1993.
3. See Jacques Derrida, 'Donner la mort', in Jean-Michel Rabaté and Michael Wetzel (eds.), *L'Ethique du don, Jacques Derrida et la pensée du don*, Paris, 1992.

only hope that he is not on the jury when one's case comes up in court.

We can note, to begin with, what an *imposing* conception of morality this is, in every sense of the word. It reworks in new language the rather antiquated idea, nowadays much under fire, that morality is mainly about imposition or obligation. But it is also imposing in the sense of being sublime, edifying, high-minded. It forgets, in other words, the sheer banality of the ethical. Like some religious thought, it sees ethics more in relation to the eternal than to the everyday. The ethical is a privileged realm in which the Other turns his luminous face to us and places upon us some inscrutable but ineluctable claim. It is an ethics bathed in an aura of religiosity – in a rhetoric of religion which has nonetheless emptied religious language of very much determinate meaning. It hijacks the halo of such thought while discarding the disreputable content, as Matthew Arnold and F. R. Leavis also did in their day.

The New Testament's view of ethics, by contrast, is distinctly irreligious. Matthew's gospel speaks of the second coming of Jesus, beginning with some familiar, reach-me-down Old Testament imagery of angels, thrones and clouds of glory. The effect, however, is one of carefully contrived bathos. What salvation comes down to is the humdrum material business of feeding the hungry, clothing the naked and visiting the sick. In typically Judaic style, salvation is an ethical matter, not a cultic one. It turns on the question of whether you have sought to protect the poor against the violence of the rich, not of how scrupulous you have been in your ritual observances. It is basically a biological affair. Even heaven is something of a let-down. The New Testament also adopts a fairly relaxed attitude to sex, and takes a notably dim view of the family.

To say that morality is basically a biological affair is to say that, like everything else about us, it is rooted ultimately in the body.[4] As Alasdair MacIntyre observes, 'Human identity is primarily, even if not only, bodily and therefore animal identity.'[5] It is the mortal, fragile, suffering, ecstatic, needy, dependent, desirous, compassionate body which furnishes the basis of all moral thought. Moral thought puts the body back into our discourse. Friedrich Nietzsche maintained that the roots of justice, prudence, bravery and moderation, indeed the whole phenomenon of morality, were essentially animal. In this sense, ethics resembles aesthetics, which started life in the mid-eighteenth century not as a language about art, but as a way of investigating bodily experience. The eighteenth century, with its cults of sentiment and sensibility, understood in its own extravagant way that moral talk was basically talk of the body. The cult of sensibility evolved a language which could cope in the same breath with the moral and the material, sympathy and the nervous system. Talk of melting, softening, swooning, palpitating, excitation and stimulation hovered ambiguously between the physical and spiritual. The nineteenth century, by contrast, was a good deal more high-minded about the whole affair.

It is because of the body, not in the first place because of Enlightenment abstraction, that we can speak of morality as universal. The material body is what we share most significantly with the whole of the rest of our species, extended both in time and space. Of course it is true that our needs, desires and sufferings are always culturally specific. But our material bodies

4. Alain Badiou's dismissal of the biological as the proper domain of ethics is one of the more questionable features of his otherwise suggestive *Ethics: An Essay on the Understanding of Evil*, London and New York, 2001.
5. Alasdair MacIntyre, *Dependent Rational Animals*, London, 1998, p. 8.

are such that they are, indeed must be, in principle capable of feeling compassion for any others of their kind. It is on this capacity for fellow-feeling that moral values are founded; and this is based in turn on our material dependency on each other. Angels, if they existed, would not be moral beings in anything like our sense.

What may persuade us that certain human bodies lack all claim on our compassion is culture. Regarding some of our fellow humans as inhuman requires a fair degree of cultural sophistication. It means having literally to disregard the testimony of our senses. This, at any rate, should give pause to those for whom 'culture' is instinctively an affirmative term. There is another sense in which culture can interpose itself between human bodies, known as technology. Technology is an extension of our bodies which can blunt their capacity to feel for one another. It is simple to destroy others at long range, but not when you have to listen to the screams. Military technology creates death but destroys the experience of it. It is easier to launch a missile attack which will wipe out thousands than run a single sentry through the guts. The painless death for which the victims have always hankered is now also prized by the perpetrators. Technology makes our bodies far more flexible and capacious, but in some ways much less responsive. It reorganizes our senses for swiftness and multiplicity rather than depth, persistence or intensity. Marx considered that by turning even our senses into commodities, capitalism had plundered us of our bodies. In his view, we would need a considerable political transformation in order to come to our senses.

Drawing parallels between humans and the other animals used to be distasteful to humanists, who insist on the unspannable gap between the two. These days it is unpalatable to culturalists. Culturalists differ from humanists in rejecting the idea of a human nature or essence; but they see eye to eye with them in maintaining a sharp distinction between language and culture on the one hand, and dumb, brute nature on the other. Alternatively, they allow culture to colonize nature from end to end, so that materiality is dissolved into meaning. In the opposite corner from both humanists and culturalists are so-called naturalists, who highlight the natural aspects of humanity and see a continuity between humans and other animals.

In fact, the link between the natural and the human, the material and the meaningful, is morality. The moral body, so to speak, is where our material nature converges with meaning and value. Both culturalists and naturalists miss this convergence from opposite ends, either underplaying or overrating the continuity between humans and their fellow creatures. In one sense, the culturalists are right: to acquire language involves a quantum leap which transfigures one's entire world, including the world of one's senses. It is not just being an animal with a linguistic bonus. Yet Alasdair MacIntyre is surely also right to insist that even as cultural beings, 'we remain animal selves with animal identities'.[6] Between the non-linguistic and the linguistic there is what one might call transformative continuity, rather as there was between the court of Charles I and that of William III, or between Baudelaire and T. S. Eliot.

We are universal animals, then, because of the kind of bodies we are born with. Stoats are a good deal more parochial. Because their bodies are not geared to complex production and communication, they are more restricted by their sensory existence than we are. Like village idiots and neighbourhood police officers, they are essentially local beings. This is absolutely no reason to patronize them. Stoats seem to do well enough in their provincial way, and

6. ibid, p. 49.

are no doubt splendid creatures in every respect. Because they are more or less confined to the immediate life of their senses, they do not go in for such abstract enterprises as constructing Cruise missiles and lobbing them at each other, unless they are being remarkably furtive about it. It is true that the 'higher', more intelligent animals can sit looser to their senses and extend their reach further beyond their bodies; but the extent to which they can do this is still meagre compared to sign-wielding beasts like ourselves. The existence of stoats is a lot more tedious than ours, but by the same token far less precarious. Because our bodies are the way they are, we can in principle enter into forms of communication far deeper and richer than physical contact with any member of our species whatsoever.

In principle, to be sure, is a vital qualification. Roughly speaking, it is culture and politics which makes it hard, and occasionally impossible, for us to do so. It is culture which is our primary source of division, as Robert Musil sardonically points out in his novel *The Man Without Qualities*: 'Admittedly they hit each other over the head and spat at each other, but they did this only because of higher cultural considerations . . .' Those today for whom culture is a buzz word, or who unequivocally celebrate cultural difference, should recall how much more peaceable human history would almost certainly have been if cultural differences had never sprung on the scene, and if the world had been almost exclusively populated by gay Chinese.

To claim, as Marx does, that individual humans share a 'species being' in common is to claim, for example, that they can conflict and conspire, kill each other for cultural or political reasons and virulently disagree. This, then, is how cosy it is to share a nature with others. We have no quarrel with stoats. Our needs may sometimes conflict with theirs, as when we destroy their natural habitat in order to bulldoze a motorway through it; but because we cannot talk to them about this, we cannot be said to disagree. Stoats cannot affirm their difference from us. They do not have the concept of difference. Only someone with whom you can communicate can affirm their difference from you. Only within some kind of common framework is conflict possible. Socialists and capitalists, or feminists and patriarchs, are not at daggers drawn if they are simply speaking about different things. Difference presupposes affinity.

The shared human nature which makes for murderous contention, however, also makes for solidarity. You cannot celebrate solidarity with a stoat. Its body is simply too different, and so therefore are the things it gets up to. You can feel sympathy for stoats, not least if some fellow human is intent on wiping them out; but you cannot strike up a deeply fulfilling, mutually satisfying relationship with them, at least not if you wish to save yourself a lot of nerve-racking visits to psychiatrists.

Human bodies are of the kind that can survive and flourish only through culture. Culture is what is natural to us. Without it we would die very quickly. Because our bodies are materially geared to culture – because meaning, symbolism, interpretation and the like are essential to what we are – we can get on terms with those from other cultures as we cannot get on terms with stoats. Because we cannot speak to stoats, their lives are eternally closed off from us. We can observe what they do, but we do not know how they make sense of it themselves. And at least one philosopher has maintained that even if such animals could speak, we would not be able to understand what they said, exactly because their bodies, and therefore their material practices, differ so radically from our own. A stoat does not have our kind of 'soul'. How do we know this? We know it by looking at what it does. A body, for example, that is not shaped so as to be able to engage in complex material production could not be said to have a human 'soul'. Stoats just don't have the paws for it.

This may not be the greatest of tragedies confronting modern humanity. There are more pressing matters to worry about than the eternal silence of the stoats. The point, however, is that humans from cultures far different from our own are in principle much more accessible than one's lovable, long-standing spaniel. This is so partly because what we share with them is just the fact that they are cultural creatures like ourselves. Being a cultural creature presupposes a whole lot of shared practices. But it is also because the kind of communication we can set up with those from different cultures, whatever the obstacles between us, is incomparably richer than our dealings with non-linguistic creatures. The very word 'understanding' is transformed when we stop talking about spaniels and start talking about Sardinians instead.

Compare, then, this materialist idea of universality, one based on our bodies, with the familiar bogeyman of universality peddled by postmodernists. On this view, universality is a Western conspiracy which speciously projects our local values and beliefs on to the entire globe. A great deal of this in fact goes on. Indeed, at the time of writing, this phoney universalism is known as George Bush. The price the West now demands of weaker, poorer cultures which wish simply to survive is that they erase their differences. To flourish, you need by and large to stop being who you are. But it is significant that when postmodernists turn their thoughts to universality, they see it first of all in terms of values and ideas. Which, as it happens, is just the way George Bush sees it too. This is an idealist, not a materialist conception of universality.

Universality today is in one sense a material fact. The aim of socialism has been to translate that fact into a value. The fact that we have become a universally communicative species – a fact which, by and large, we have capitalism to thank for – should lay the basis for a global order in which the needs of every individual can be satisfied. The global village must become the co-operative commonwealth. But this is not just a moral prescription. 'Ought' implies 'can': the very resources which have brought a global existence into being have also made possible in principle a new form of political existence. Such a life, Marxists have traditionally insisted, is no longer an idle dream, as it would have been in 1500. Just because of some of the technologies developed by capitalism, we now have the material basis on which it might be realized. In fact, if we do not realize it we might end up with no material basis at all. Once everyone can be in on the political act, furnished with a sufficiency of spiritual and material goods, we can expect conflict, argument, difference and dissent to thrive. For one thing, there would be a great many more people able to articulate their views and gain a public hearing. The situation would be exactly the opposite of some anodyne utopia.

Spurious kinds of universality insist that we are all the same. But from whose standpoint? They eradicate differences, but only to reinstate them as conflicts. Eradicating differences is a violent business, and those whose identities are imperilled by it tend to respond in much the same bloodstained coin. Genuine kinds of universality, however, understand that difference belongs to our common nature. It is not the opposite of it. The body may be the fundamental way that we belong to each other, but it is also the way in which we are uniquely individuated. To encounter another human body is thus to encounter, indissociably, both sameness and difference. The body of the other is at once strange and familiar. It is exactly the fact that we can relate to it which highlights its otherness. Other things in the world are not strange to us in the same sense at all.

Individuation is one of the activities proper to our species being. It is a practice, not a given condition. It is something that we do, as we come to negotiate a unique identity for ourselves in the very media that we share in common. Being an individual human being is not like being an individual peach. It is a project we have to accomplish. It is an autonomy we forge for ourselves on the basis of our shared existence, and thus a function of our dependency rather than an alternative to it. Our species life is such that it enables us to establish a unique relationship to the species known as personal identity. Matter is always a particular business: it is always this specific bit of the stuff, not just any old stuff. The word 'specific' itself means both peculiar and 'of the species'.

For present-day cultural theory, all such properly zoological talk of human beings as a natural species is profoundly suspect. Since humanism – a belief in the unique status of human beings within Nature – is no longer much in fashion, the task of safeguarding human supremacy has passed instead to culturalism. Culturalism is the form of reductionism which sees everything in cultural terms, as economism sees everything in economic terms. It is thus uncomfortable with the truth that we are, among other things, natural material objects or animals, and insists instead that our material nature is culturally constructed.

To convert the whole world into culture is one way of disavowing its independence of us, and thus of disowning the possibility of our death. If the world depends for its reality on our discourse about it, then this seems to lend the human animal, however 'decentred', an imposing centrality. It makes our existence appear less contingent, more ontologically solid, and so less of a prey to mortality. We are the precious custodians of meaning, since we are all that stands between reality and utter chaos. It is we who give tongue to the dumb things around us. Culturalism is of course right that a natural event like death can be signified in a myriad cultural styles. But we die anyway. Death represents Nature's final victory over culture. The fact that it is culturally signified does not stop it from being a non-contingent part of our creaturely nature. It is our perishing, not our bestowals of meaning, which is necessary. The dumb things around us fared perfectly well before we happened upon the scene. Indeed, they were not at that time dumb at all, since it is only we who define them as mute. Death, however, which sketches an intolerable limit to the omnipotent will, is too indecent an event to be much spoken of in the society (the United States) from which a good deal of culturalist thought springs, which may be one reason why such thought can prosper there.

Culturalists are afraid that unless we keep reminding ourselves that we are cultural animals, we will slip back into the insidious habit of 'naturalizing' our existence, treating ourselves as unalterable beings. Hence their protests against essentialism, which would have been much commended by such doyens of bourgeois thought as John Locke and Jeremy Bentham. In fact, one can be just as essentialist about culture as one can be about Nature. In any case, this case sometimes appears to assume that all permanence is objectionable and all change desirable, which is absurd. There are many reasonably permanent features of human existence which we have cause to be grateful for, and many sorts of change which are destructive.

Change is not desirable in itself, whatever the postmodern advocates of perpetual plasticity may consider. Nor is it undesirable in itself. One can be moved by the laconic pathos of W. B. Yeats's lament, 'Man is in love, and loves what vanishes, What more is there to say?' Yet there are many things, from plague to patriarchy, which cannot vanish quickly enough. There are also a good many aspects of our condition which we cannot in fact change, without our needing to feel especially dispirited about it. That human beings are always and everywhere social animals is an unchanging fact, but scarcely a tragic one. Much permanence is to be celebrated. The long-standing tradition that academics over the age of fifty are not automatically put to the sword is a cause for rejoicing, for some of us if not for others. In any case, if some ideology makes the historical appear natural, by no means all ideology does so. Some of it does just the opposite, triumphantly making Nature seem mere clay in our hands.

It is extraordinary that citizens of the contemporary West could imagine that overlooking the changeability of things is one of our greatest perils. On the contrary, there is far too much change around, not too little. Whole ways of life are wiped out almost overnight. Men and women must scramble frantically to acquire new skills or be thrown on the scrapheap. Technology becomes obsolete in its infancy and monstrously swollen corporations threaten to implode. All that is solid – banks, pensions schemes, anti-arms treaties, obese newspaper magnates – melts into air. Human identities are shucked off, reshuffled, tried on for size, tilted at a roguish angle and flamboyantly paraded along the catwalks of social life. In the midst of this perpetual agitation, one sound middle-aged reason for being a socialist is to take a breather.

The body, that inconvenient reminder of mortality, is plucked, pierced, etched, pummelled, pumped up, shrunk and remoulded. Flesh is converted into sign, staving off the moment when it will subside into the sheer pornographic meaninglessness of a corpse. Dead bodies are indecent: they proclaim with embarrassing candour the secret of all matter, that it has no obvious relation to meaning. The moment of death is the moment when meaning haemorrhages from us. What seems a celebration of the body, then, may also cloak a virulent anti-materialism – a desire to gather this raw, perishable stuff into the less corruptible forms of art or discourse. The resurrection of the body returns as the tattoo parlour and the cosmetic surgeon's consulting-room. To reduce this obstreperous stuff to so much clay in our hands is a fantasy of mastering the unmasterable. It is a disavowal of death, a refusal of the limit which is ourselves.

Capitalism, too, for all its crass materialism, is secretly allergic to matter. No individual object can fulfil its voracious appetite, as it hunts its way restlessly from one to the other, dissolving each of them to nothing in doomed pursuit of its ultimate desire. For all its love affair with matter, in the shape of Tuscan villas and double brandies, capitalist society harbours a secret hatred of the stuff. It is a culture shot through with fantasy, idealist to its core, powered by a disembodied will which dreams of pounding Nature to pieces. It makes an idol out of matter, but cannot stomach the resistance it offers to its grandiose schemes.

It is, to be sure, no crime to tattoo your biceps. The West has long believed in moulding Nature to its own desires; it is just that it used to be known as the pioneer spirit and is nowadays known as postmodernism. Taming the Mississippi and piercing your navel are just earlier and later versions of the same ideology. Having moulded the landscape to our own image and likeness, we have now begun to recraft ourselves. Civil engineering has been joined by cosmetic surgery. But there can be more and less creditable reasons for piercing your navel. The creditable reason is that it is fun; the discreditable reason is that it may involve the belief that your body, like your bank account, is yours to do what you like with. There may be excellent reasons to sport a vulture on your chest or a steel bolt through your nose, but this is not one of them.

'Personalizing' the body may be a way of denying its essential impersonality. Its impersonality lies in the fact that it belongs to the species before it belongs to me; and there are some aspects of the species-body – death, vulnerability, sickness and the like – that we may well prefer to thrust into oblivion. Even then, there is no very coherent sense in which my body belongs to me. It is not a possession, like a scarlet fez or a mobile phone. Who would be the possessor? It sounds odd to call a 'possession' something which I never acquired and could never give away. I am not the proprietor of my sensations. Having a painful twinge is not like having a tweed cap. I could give you my cap, but not my twinge. I can call my body 'mine', but this is to mark the distinction between my body and yours, not to indicate that I am the owner of it. There is no private entrepreneurship when it comes to flesh and blood.

The body is the most palpable sign we have of the givenness of human existence. It is not something we get to choose. My body is not something I decided to walk around in, like a toupee. It is not something I am 'in' at all. Having a body is not like being inside a tank. Who would be this disembodied 'I' inside it? It is more like having a language. Having a language, as we have seen, is not like being trapped in a tank or a prison house; it is a way of being in the midst of a world. To be on the 'inside' of a language is to have a world opened up to you, and thus to be on the 'outside' of it at the same time. The same is true of the human body. Having a body is a way of going to work on the world, not a way of being walled off from it. It would be odd to complain that I could come at things better if only I could shuck off my flesh. It would be like complaining that I could talk to you better if only this crude, ineffectual stuff called speech did not get in the way.

The fact that my body is not one of my possessions does not give you *carte blanche* to muscle in on it. You cannot possess it either. But this is not because I got there first, like a piece of lucrative land to which I staked the first claim. Part of the point of bodies is their anonymity. We are intimate with our bodies, but we cannot grasp them as a whole. There is always a kind of 'outside' to my body, which I can only ever squint at sideways. The body is my way of being present to others in ways which are bound in part to elude me. It slips through my grasp, just as it does when it asserts its own stubborn material logic in the face of my hubristic schemes. In all of these ways, its mortality is revealed – for nothing is at once more intimate and more alien to us than death. My death is *my* death, already secreted in my bones, stealthily at work in my body; yet it leaps upon my life and extinguishes it as though from some other dimension. It is always untimely.

The impersonality of the body is related to the anonymity of love. Love here has its traditional sense of *agape* or charity, not the impoverished meaning which narrows it to the erotic or Romantic variety of the stuff. We need a term somewhere between the intensity of 'love' and the rather cooler 'friendship', and the fact that we lack one is probably significant. Love is no respecter of persons. It is remorselessly abstract, ready to attend to the needs of any old body. In this, it is quite indifferent to cultural difference. It is not indifferent to difference in the sense that it is blind to the *specific* needs of people. If it was, it would not be attending to *them* at all. But it is quite indifferent as to whose specific needs it attends to. This is one way in which it differs from friendship, which is all about particularity. Friends are irreplaceable, but those we must love are not. Love is also indifferent in the sense of being unilateral and unconditional. It does not give on the assumption that it will receive. It is unresponsive, too, in the sense that it does not repay injury with injury. This is one reason why it is sometimes hard to distinguish from cynicism, which is so detached from what it sees as the whole farcical business of human value that it does not even see much point in retaliation.

All this is why the paradigm of love is not the love of friends –
what could be less demanding? – but the love of strangers. If love
is not just to be an imaginary affair, a mutual mirroring of egos,
it has to attend to that in the other which is deeply strange, in
the sense of being fearful and recalcitrant. It is a matter of loving
that 'inhuman' thing in the other which lies also at the core of
ourselves. We have to love ourselves, too, in all of our squalor
and recalcitrance, if self-love is to be more than self-admiration.
This is why loving others as oneself is by no means as simple as
it sounds. Indeed, both activities are perhaps beyond our power.
They are, however, what it would take to redeem the ravages of
desire, which is likewise impersonal, and which installs itself like
a monster at the heart of the self. Desire is nothing personal. Only
a correspondingly impersonal force would be capable of undoing
the frightful damage which it wreaks.

Aristotle's man of virtue is notoriously self-centred. He enjoys
friendship as part of the good life, but it is the life of contemplation
he finds most precious. What Aristotle does not fully appreciate is
that virtue is a reciprocal affair. He sees, to be sure, that it can
thrive only in political society; but he does not really recognize
that virtue is what happens between people – that it is a function
of relationships. His so-called 'great-souled man' is alarmingly
self-sufficient. Friendship matters to the man of virtue, but it is more
mutual admiration than genuine love. As Alasdair MacIntyre puts it:
'For the love of the person, as against the goodness, pleasantness, or
usefulness of the person, Aristotle can have no place.'[7]

The opposite of self-sufficiency is dependency. Like some other
key terms, as we shall see in a moment, this hovers somewhere
between the material and the moral. It is a material fact that we
are dependent on others for our physical survival, given the helpless

7. Alasdair MacIntyre, *A Short History of Ethics*, London, 1968, p. 80.

state in which we are born. Yet this material dependency cannot really be divorced from such moral capacities as care, selflessness, vigilance and protectiveness, since what we are dependent on is exactly such capacities in those who look after us. Nor, according to Freud, can it be divorced from the dawning of moral feeling in the dependent one, in the form of gratitude. We shall literally not become persons, as opposed to being human animals, unless those whom we bank on share something of their affective and communicative life with us. To this extent, the moral and material are sides of the same coin.

Aristotelian Man, remarks MacIntyre, is a stranger to love. Yet love is the very model of a just society, even if the word has these days become faintly ridiculous when used in anything but interpersonal terms. Love means creating for another the kind of space in which he can flourish, at the same time as he does this for you. It is to find one's happiness in being the reason for the happiness of another. It is not that you both find your fulfilment in the same goal, like hitting the open road clasped together on a motor-cycle, but, as we have seen already, that you each find your fulfilment in the other's. There is already a politics implicit in this notion, as we have noted. The liberal model of society wants individuals to flourish in their own space, without mutual interference. The political space in question is thus a neutral one: it is really there to wedge people apart, so that one person's self-realization should not thwart another's.[8]

8. A contemporary example of this would be the work of Jurgen Habermas. In Habermas's public sphere, each person is free to express herself as she wishes; but there is little recognition of the way in which social interaction itself can become the vital medium of individual self-expression at its best. Nobody here – to put the point in a different theoretical idiom – seems to receive themselves back as a subject from the Other, as opposed to attending with due sensitivity to what the other has to say.

This is an admirable ideal, nurtured by what is in many ways a deeply honourable political tradition. The 'negative' freedoms it cherishes have a vital place in any just society. But the space involved in love is rather more positive. It is created by the act of relationship itself, rather than being given from the outset like a spare seat in a waiting-room. To be granted this kind of freedom is to be able to be at one's best without undue fear. It is thus the vital precondition of human flourishing. You are free to realize your nature, but not in the falsely naturalistic sense of simply expressing an impulse because it happens to be yours. That would not rule out torture and murder. Rather, you realize your nature in a way which allows the other to do so too. And that means that you realize your nature at its best – since if the other's self-fulfilment is the medium through which you flourish yourself, you are not at liberty to be violent, dominative or self-seeking.

The political equivalent of this situation, as we have seen, is known as socialism. When Aristotle's ethics of flourishing are set in a more interactive context, one comes up with something like the political ethics of Marx. The socialist society is one in which each attains his or her freedom and autonomy in and through the self-realization of others. Socialism is just whatever set of institutions it would take for it to happen. One can see, too, why equality is a key concept for socialist thought. For you cannot really have this process of reciprocal self-realization except among equals. Strictly speaking, equality is not necessary for love. You can love your children, for example, or your hamster. Some people even love their bedroom slippers. But equality is necessary for what Aristotle calls *philia*, or friendship; and this, rather than love, is perhaps the more appropriate political term. There cannot be full friendship between non-equals. We may feel too constrained in the presence of a superior to express ourselves fully and freely, while the superior may be stymied by his need to preserve his authority. Only a relationship of equality can create individual autonomy. It is not that there are two autonomous individuals who then enter into an equal relationship. Rather, it is the equality which allows them to be autonomous. Friendship frees you to be yourself.

In his early Paris Manuscripts, Marx was seeking for a way of moving from how it is with the human body to how it ought to be. He wanted an ethics and politics based on our species-being or shared material nature. But this is a notoriously perilous enterprise. Philosophers have generally placed a ban on such attempts to derive values from facts. A straight description of a situation will not tell you what you should do about it. Human nature can be described in a rich diversity of ways, and there can be all sorts of competing versions of it to back up different ethical theories. 'Nature' is a slippery term, gliding between fact (how it is with something) and value (how it should be). It shares this ambiguity with the word 'culture', which some see as the opposite of Nature. We have, in fact, a whole vocabulary which links bodily states with moral ones: kind, tender, unfeeling, touched, touchy, thick-skinned, insensitive and the like. This language seems to imply a connection between how it is with the body and how we should or should not behave. But it is a connection plagued with problems. Being 'kind', in the sense of being of the same species as another, is often enough a reason for killing or being killed, dominating or being subjugated. If we were not 'kind', we might be treated a lot better. Nobody is particularly interested in subjugating beetles.

Or take the idea of human sociality. It, too, is suspended somewhere between fact and value. It is a fact that we are naturally political animals, at home only in society. Unless we co-operated with each other, we could not survive. But sociality can also mean an active, positive form of co-operation, something which is desirable rather than just biologically inevitable. Marx sometimes seems to imagine that sociality is always positive in this way. But a fascist society is also a co-operative one. The death camps were a complex collaborative project. There is a good deal of solidarity between the members of the World Bank. There is no virtue in human co-operation in itself. It depends on who is co-operating with whom for what purpose. Marx sees how some men and women can hijack the social capacities of others for their own selfish purposes. For him, indeed, this is a description of class society. In class society, even those powers and capabilities which belong to us as a species – labour, for example, or communication – are degraded into means to an end. They become instrumentalized for the advantage of others. One can say much the same about sexual life. Sexuality is a medium of solidarity which in patriarchal society becomes a means of power, dominion and selfish satisfaction.

But what if you are not co-operating over anything in particular? You need, of course, to work together to survive economically. Sexuality is necessary if the species is to be reproduced. Co-operation generally has some sort of practical goal. But what if it is enjoyed at the same time as an end in itself? What if the sharing of life becomes its own purpose, rather as in the activity we know as art? You do not need to find an answer to why human beings live together and enjoy each others' company – some of the time, at least. It is in their nature to do so. It is a fact about them as animals. But when it becomes 'fully' a fact – when it exists as an activity in itself, not simply as a means to an end beyond it – it also becomes a source of value. A socialist society co-operates for certain material purposes, just like any other; but it also regards human solidarity as an estimable end in itself. As such, it is beyond the comprehension of a good deal of contemporary cultural theory, for which solidarity means tepid consensus or baleful conformism rather than a source of value and fulfilment.

7

Revolution, Foundations
and Fundamentalists

We have seen that for some cultural thinkers, ethics should be hoisted from the banal realm of the biological into something altogether more enigmatic and mysterious. From this viewpoint, there cannot really be a materialist ethics. Yet Derrida, Lyotard, Badiou and their colleagues are also in a sense right. The ethical is indeed about momentous, life-changing encounters as well as about everyday life. It is clouds of glory *and* feeding the hungry. It is just that these thinkers opt on the whole for the sublime rather than the sublunary. But the two go together, since fashioning a world in which the hungry could be fed would require a dramatic transformation. As Theodor Adorno remarks: 'There is tenderness only in the coarsest demand: that no-one should go hungry any more.'[1]

Take, for example, a revolutionary document like the Book of Isaiah. The poet who wrote this book opens with a typically anti-religious bout of irascibility on the part of Yahweh, the Jewish God. Yahweh tells his people that he is fed up with their solemn assemblies and sacrificial offerings ('incense is an abomination to me'), and counsels them instead to 'seek justice, correct oppression, defend the fatherless, plead for the widow'.

1. Theodor Adorno, *Minima Moralia*, London, 1974, p. 156.

174

This is standard Old Testament stuff. Yahweh is forever having to remind his pathologically cultic people that salvation is a political affair, not a religious one. He himself is a non-god, a god of the 'not yet', one who signifies a social justice which has not yet arrived, and who cannot even be named for fear that he will be turned into just another fetish by his compulsively idolatrous devotees. He is not to be bound to the pragmatic needs and interests of the status quo. He will be known for what he is, so he informs his people, when they see the stranger being made welcome, the hungry being filled with good things, and the rich being sent empty away.

Words like these were to become a set-piece chant among some of the underground revolutionaries of politically turbulent first-century Palestine, and Luke puts them into the mouth of Mary when she hears that she is pregnant with Jesus. The people, for their part, prefer the solace of organized religion to the business of feeding the hungry. This is why they are denounced by prophets like Isaiah. The role of the prophet is not to predict the future, but to remind the people that if they carry on as they are doing, the future will be exceedingly bleak.

For the so-called Old Testament, the non-god Yahweh and the 'non-being' of the poor are closely connected. Indeed, it is the first historical document to forge such a relationship. In a revolutionary reversal, true power springs from powerlessness. As St Paul writes in Corinthians: 'God chose what is weakest in the world to shame the strong . . . even things that are not, to bring to nothing things that are.' The whole of Judaeo-Christian thought is cast in this ironic, paradoxical, up-ending mould. The wretched of the earth are known to the Old Testament as the *anawim*, those whose desperate plight embodies the failure of the political order. The only valid image of the future is the failure of the present. The *anawim*, who are the favoured children of Yahweh, have no stake in the current set-up, and so are an image of the future in their very destitution. The dispossessed are a living sign of the truth that the only enduring power is one anchored in an acknowledgement of failure. Any power which fails to recognize this fact will be enfeebled in a different sense, fearfully defending itself against the victims of its own arrogance. Here, as often, paranoia has much to recommend it. The exercise of power is child's play compared to the confession of weakness. Power can destroy whole cities, but there is nothing very remarkable in that. Destroying whole cities is a relatively simple business.

The authors of the New Testament see Jesus as a type of the *anawim*. He is dangerous because he has no stake in the present set-up. Those who speak up for justice will be done away with by the state. Society will wreak its terrible vengeance on the vulnerable. The only good God is a dead one – a failed political criminal in an obscure corner of the earth. There can be no success which does not keep faith with failure. It is this faith which has since been used to justify imperialist adventures, the repression of women, the disembowelling of unbelievers, the reviling of Jews, the abuse of children and the murder of abortionists. As a form of organized violence, it has become the badge of the rich, powerful and patriotic. It is the nauseating cant of US Evangelists, the joyous cries of bomb-happy militarists washed in the blood of the Lamb, and the suburban respectability of fraudsters and wife-beaters. It is glazed, bland, beaming and tambourine-banging. It wants nothing to do with failure, and shoos the *anawim* off the streets. It is the logo of the military-industrial complex, the cross which props up the American Eagle, the holy water sprinkled on human exploitation.

At the same time, much atheism today is just inverted religion. Atheists tend to advance a version of religion which nobody in their right mind would subscribe to, and then righteously reject it. They accept the sort of crude stereotypes of it that would no doubt horrify them in any other field of scholarly inquiry. They are rather like those for whom feminism means penis-envy, or socialism labour camps. A card-carrying atheist like Richard Dawkins is in this respect the mere mirror-image of Ian Paisley. Both see Yahweh as (in William Blake's word) Nobodaddy, which in the Old Testament itself is a Satanic image of God. It is the image of God of those who want an authoritarian superego or Celestial Manufacturer to worship or revolt against.

This God is also a wizard entrepreneur, having economized on his materials by manufacturing the universe entirely out of nothing. Like a temperamental rock star, he fusses over minor matters of diet, and like an irascible dictator demands constant placating and cajoling. He is a cross between a Mafia boss and a prima donna, with nothing to be said in his favour other than that he is, when all is said and done, God. It is just that the atheist rejects this image while the Evangelical accepts it. Otherwise, they are pretty much at one. The real challenge is to construct a version of religion which is actually *worth* rejecting. And this has to start from countering your opponent's best case, not her worst.

This is as true of Islam as it is of Judaeo-Christianity. Islam first emerged as a radical critique of the injustice and inequality of an aggressively commercialist Mecca, in which the old, egalitarian tribal values of caring for the weaker members of the community were giving way to the profit motive. The word *Quaran*, which means 'recital', indicates the illiterate status of most of Muhammad's early followers. The very title of the Muslim scriptures suggests poverty and deprivation. *Islam*, which means 'surrender', suggests a total self-dedication to the Allah whose gospel is one of mercy, equality, compassion and a championship of the poor. The Muslim body itself had to be re-educated in such postures as prostration out of the arrogance and self-sufficiency

177

which were growing apace in Mecca society. Muslims must fast throughout Ramadan, as Christians do throughout Lent, to remind themselves of the privations of the poor. Non-violence, community and social justice lie at the heart of Islamic faith, which is notably averse to theological speculation. As with Christianity, the distinction between sacred and profane, the sublime and the mundane, is dismantled. No clerical class in the Christian sense is permitted, to emphasize the equality of all believers. It is this admirable creed which has become in our own time the doctrine of oil-rich autocrats and the stoners of women, fascist-minded mullahs and murderous bigots.

The Book of Isaiah is strong stuff for these post-revolutionary days. It is only left in hotel rooms because nobody bothers to read it. If those who deposit it there had any idea what it contained, they would be well advised to treat it like pornography and burn it on the spot. As far as revolution goes, the human species divides between those who see the world as containing pockets of misery in an ocean of increasing well-being, and those who see it as containing pockets of well-being in an ocean of increasing misery. It also divides between those who agree with Schopenhauer that it would probably have been better for a great many people in history if they had never been born, and those who regard this as lurid leftist hyperbole. This, in the end, is perhaps the only political division which really counts. It is far more fundamental than that between Jews and Muslims, Christians and atheists, men and women or liberals and communitarians. It is the kind of conflict in which it takes a strenuous act of imagination for each party to understand how the other can believe what it does. This is not always the case with disagreement. You can disagree that broccoli is delicious or that Dorking is the most vibrant town in Europe while being able to imagine quite easily what it would be like to agree.

Radicals do not reject the ocean-of-well-being theory because they reject the reality of progress. Only conservatives and post-modernists do that. In certain postmodern quarters, the word 'progress' is greeted with the withering scorn usually reserved for those who believe that the face of Elvis Presley keeps mysteriously showing up on chocolate chip cookies. Those who are sceptical of progress, however, do not generally turn up their noses at dental anaesthetics or signal their exasperation when clean water gushes from the tap. What we might call Big Bang conservatives tend to believe that everything has being going to the dogs since a golden age, whereas for Steady State conservatives even the golden age wasn't all it is cracked up to be. For them, the snake was always-already curled ominously in the garden. It is logically dubious whether one can backslide all the time, but some conservatives appear undeterred by this difficulty. Some of them seem to maintain that all historical periods are equally corrupt, and that the past was superior to the present. T. S. Eliot's *The Waste Land* can be read as holding both beliefs simultaneously.

Postmodernists reject the idea of progress because they are distracted by grand narratives. They assume that a belief in progress must entail that history as a whole has been steadily on the up from the outset, a view which they naturally dismiss as a delusion. If they were less taken with grand narratives they might follow their own lights, take a more pragmatic attitude to progress, and arrive at the correct but boring conclusion that human history has improved in some respects while deteriorating in others. Marxism tries to make this tattered cliché sound less banal by pointing out, more imaginatively, that the progress and the deterioration are closely linked aspects of the same narrative. The conditions which make for emancipation also make for domination.

This is known as dialectical thought. Modern history has been an enlightened tale of material welfare, liberal values, civil rights, democratic politics and social justice, and an atrocious nightmare. These two fables are by no means unrelated. The condition of the poor is intolerable partly because the resources to alleviate it exist in abundance. Starvation is appalling partly because it is unnecessary. Social change is necessary because of the lamentable state of the planet, but also possible because of material advances. Postmodernists, however, who pride themselves on their pluralism, prefer to consider the question of progress more one-sidedly.

In one sense, the need for revolution is plain realism. No enlightened, moderately intelligent observer could survey the state of the planet and conclude that it could be put to rights without a thorough-going transformation. To this extent, it is the hard-nosed pragmatists who are the dewy-eyed dreamers, not the wild-haired leftists. They are really just sentimentalists of the status quo. To speak of thorough-going transformation, however, is to say nothing about what form that change might take. Revolutions are characterized by how deep-seated they are, not how swift, bloody or sudden. Some processes of piecemeal reform have involved more violence than some armed insurrections. The revolutions which produced us took several centuries to complete. They were made not in the name of a utopian future, but because of the deficiencies of the present.

As Walter Benjamin remarked, it is memories of enslaved ancestors, not dreams of liberated grandchildren, which drive men and women to revolt. This, in short, is the radical version of the well-known query: What has posterity ever done for us? Nobody in their senses would suffer the disruptions of radical change in the name of some intriguing theoretical experiment.

As with the fall of apartheid or the toppling of Communism, such changes are made only when they need to be. It is when a feasible alternative to the present regime is unlikely to be more dire than the regime itself that people may arrive at the eminently rational decision not to carry on as they are doing.

Like the spotty, overweight and paralytically shy, radicals would rather not be the way they are. They regard themselves as holding awkward, mildly freakish opinions forced upon them by the current condition of the species, and yearn secretly to be normal. Or rather, they look forward to a future in which they would no longer be saddled with such inconvenient beliefs, since they would have been been realized in practice. They would then be free to join the rest of the human race. It is not pleasant to be continually out of line. It is also paradoxical that those who believe in the sociality of human existence should be forced on this very account to live against the grain. To the cheerleaders for Life, it seems unwarrantably ascetic. They do not see that the asceticism, if that is what it is, is in the name of a more abundant life for everyone. Radicals are simply those who recognize, in Yeats's words, that 'Nothing can be sole or whole / That has not been rent.' It is not their fault that this is so. They would rather that it was not.

Let us look once again at the idea of a materialist morality, this time as illustrated by Shakespeare's *King Lear*. Lear begins the play by exemplifying the megalomania of absolute sovereignty, which imagines that it is omnipotent partly because it has no body. In casting off so cruelly the fruits of his body, his daughter Cordelia, he discloses the fantasy of disembodiment which lies at the heart of the most grossly material of powers. Lear believes at this point that he is everything; but since an identity which is everything has nothing to measure itself against, it is merely a void. Similarly, a nation which becomes global in its sovereignty will soon have very little idea of who it is, if indeed it ever knew. It has eliminated the otherness which is essential for self-knowledge.

In the course of the drama, Lear will learn that it is preferable to be a modestly determinate 'something' than a vacuously global 'all'. This is not because others tell him so, being for the most part too craven or crafty to respond to his tormented question, 'Who is it that can tell me who I am?' It is because he is forced up against the brute recalcitrance of Nature, which reminds him pitilessly of what all absolute power is likely to forget, namely that he has a body. Nature terrorizes him into finally embracing his own finitude. And this includes his creaturely compassion for others. It therefore redeems him from delusion, if not from destruction.

The play opens with a celebrated bandying of nothings:

> LEAR: . . . what can you say to draw
>   A third more opulent than your sisters? Speak.
> CORDELIA: Nothing, my lord.
> LEAR: Nothing!
> CORDELIA: Nothing.
> LEAR: Nothing will come of nothing. Speak again.
>   (Act 1, scene 1)

Despite Lear's irascible finger-wagging, something does finally come of nothing, or almost nothing. Only when this paranoid monarch accepts that he stinks of mortality will he be *en route* to redemption. It is then that his lying courtiers will be discredited:

> To say 'ay' and 'no' to everything that I said! 'Ay' and 'no' too was no good divinity. When the rain came to wet me once, and the wind to make me chatter; when the thunder would not peace

at my bidding; there I found 'em, there I smelt 'em out. Go to, they are not men of their words. They told me I was everything; 'tis a lie – I am not ague-proof.

(Act 4, scene 6)

The storm has thrown Lear's creatureliness into exposure, deflating his hubristic fantasies. He has discovered his flesh for the first time, and along with it his frailty and finitude. Gloucester will do the same when he is blinded, forced to 'smell his way to Dover'. He must learn, as he says, to 'see feelingly' – to allow his reason to move within the constraints of the sensitive, suffering body. When we are out of our body, we are out of our mind.

Lear's new-found sensuous materialism takes the form of a political solidarity with the poor:

Poor naked wretches, wheresoe'er you are,
That bide the pelting of this pitiless storm,
How shall your houseless heads and unfed sides,
Your loop'd and window'd raggedness, defend you
From seasons such as these? O, I have ta'en
Too little care of this! Take physic, pomp;
Expose thyself to feel what wretches feel,
That thou mayst shake the superflux to them,
And show the heavens more just.

(Act 3, scene 4)

If power had a body, it would be forced to abdicate. It is because it is fleshless that it fails to feel the misery it inflicts. What blunts its senses is a surplus of material property. If it has no body of its own, it nevertheless has a kind of surrogate

183

flesh, a thick, fat-like swaddling of material possessions, which insulate it against compassion:

> Let the superfluous and lust-dieted man
> That slaves your ordinance, that does not see
> Because he does not feel, feel your power quickly;
> So distribution should undo excess,
> And each man have enough.
>
> (Act 4, scene 1)

If our sympathy for others were not so sensuously depleted, we would be moved by their deprivation to share with them the very goods which prevent us from feeling their wretchedness. The problem could thus become the solution. The renewal of the body and a radical redistribution of wealth are closely linked. To perceive accurately, we must feel; and to feel we need to free the body from the anaesthesia which too much property imposes on it. The rich are insulated from fellow feeling by an excess of property, whereas what impoverishes the bodies of the poor is too little of it. For the rich to repair their own sensory deprivation would be for them to feel for the privations of others. And the result of this would be a radical social change, not just a change of heart. In Shakespeare's imagination, communism and corporeality are closely allied.

The trouble with the rich is that property binds you to the present and thereby cocoons you from death. The rich need to live more provisionally, and the poor more securely. The ideal combination would be to live with a sufficiency of goods but to be prepared to give them up. This is notably hard to achieve; but such sacrifice is in fact what everyone is forced to in the end, in the form of death. Being prepared to let it go right now makes death less terrible when it comes along. If we have grown used to living with lack, refusing to stuff our desire with idols and fetishes, we have rehearsed for death in life, and so have made it seem less fearful. Self-giving in life is a rehearsal for the final self-abandonment of death. It is this that the rich find hard to do. The problem is that as long as the rich exist, the poor cannot live abundantly, and as long as the poor exist, the rich cannot live provisionally. They will need constantly to watch their backs.

Property deprives you of a genuine future. It ensures that the future will be simply an endless repetition of the present. The future for the well-heeled will be just like the present, only more so. One's deepest hope is that nothing momentous will ever happen. When asked what they fear most, the rich can reply in the words of a former British prime minister: 'Events, dear boy, events.' It is fear, rather than hatred, which lies at the root of most human mischief, not least at the root of hatred. The rich need more discontinuity in their lives, while the poor need more stability. The rich have no future because they have too much present, whereas the poor have no future because they have too little present. Neither can thus recount a satisfactory narrative of themselves.

The West, and in particular the United States, has not, by and large, learnt the lesson of Lear. The USA is a nation which tends to find failure shameful, mortifying or even downright sinful. What distinguishes its culture is its buoyancy, its robust exuberance, its doggone refusal to cave in, cop out or say 'can't'. It is a nation of eager yea-sayers and zealous can-doers, in contrast with that bunch of professional grousers, scoffers and long-suffering stoics known as the British. No group of people uses the word 'dream' so often, except for psychoanalysts. American culture is deeply hostile to the idea of limit, and therefore to human biology. Postmodernism is obsessed by the body and terrified of biology.

The body is a wildly popular topic in US cultural studies – but this is the plastic, remouldable, socially constructed body, not the piece of matter that sickens and dies. Because death is the absolute failure to which we all eventually come, it has not been the most favoured of topics for discussion in the United States. The US distributors of the British film *Four Weddings and a Funeral* fought hard, if unsuccessfully, to change the title.

In such a culture there can be no real tragedy, whatever terrifying events may occur from time to time. The United States is a profoundly anti-tragic society which is now having to confront what may well prove the most terrible epoch of its history. For tragedy, like its partner comedy, depends on an acknowledgement of the flawed, botched nature of human life – though in tragedy one has to be hauled through hell to arrive at this recognition, so obdurate and tenacious is human self-delusion. Comedy embraces roughness and imperfection from the outset, and has no illusions about pious ideals. Against such grandiose follies, it pits the lowly, persistent, indestructible stuff of everyday life. Nobody can take a tragic tumble because nobody is that uniquely precious anyway.

Tragic protagonists, by contrast, need to be bound to a wheel of fire before they can be brought to acknowledge that flawedness is part of the texture of things, and that roughness and imprecision are what make human life work. As a form, tragedy is still in thrall to the harshly unforgiving superego – to cruelly demanding ideals which simply rub our noses in our failure to live up to them. At the same time, unlike comedy, it understands that not all ideals are a sham. If tragedy risks crediting such lofty notions too much, comedy risks a certain populist cynicism about them. Tragedy is about wresting victory from failure, whereas comedy concerns the victory of failure itself, the way in which a wry sharing and acceptance of our weaknesses makes us much less killable.

In tragedy, much turns on the fact that we are not wholly masters of our own destiny. It is this which is hard to stomach in an American culture for which 'I've made my choices' is a familiar phrase, and 'It wasn't my fault' an unacceptable one. It is this doctrine which has put so many on death row. In jaded, death-ridden Europe it is harder to overlook the great mounds of historical rubble in which the self is buried, and which cramp its liberty to become whatever it chooses. Cynicism, rather than square-jawed idealism, is thus more in fashion there. If the USA is the land of will-power, Europe is the home of Nietzsche's will to power, which in some ways is almost the opposite.

What is immortal in the United States, what refuses to lie down and die, is precisely the will. Like desire, there's always more will where that came from. But whereas desire is hard to dominate, the will is dominion itself. It is a terrifyingly uncompromising drive, one which knows no faltering or bridling, irony or self-doubt. It is so greedy for the world that it is at risk of pounding it to pieces in its sublime fury, cramming it into its insatiable maw. The will is apparently in love with all it sees, but is secretly in love with itself. It is not surprising that it often enough takes on a military form, since the death drive lurks within it. Its virile vigour conceals a panic-stricken disavowal of death. It has the hubris of all claims to self-sufficiency.

This annihilating will finds its reflection in the voluntaristic clichés of American culture: the sky's the limit, never say never, you can crack it if you have faith in yourself. If the disabled do not walk, at least they can redesignate themselves as challenged. As with all pieces of ideology too loosely hinged to the real world – 'life is sacred', 'all human beings are special', 'the best things in life are free' – these solemn soundbites are believed and disbelieved at the same time. Ideology, like the Freudian unconscious, is a domain untouched by the law which prohibits contradiction. As long as the frenetically active will is in business, there can be no finality, and hence no tragedy. The cult of the will belongs with a callow, kitschy optimism, full of wide-eyed vision and the swooping of violins.

In this remorselessly up-beat climate, feeling negative becomes a thought-crime, and satire a form of political treason. Everyone is urged to feel good about themselves, whereas the problem is that some of them don't feel anything like bad enough. Evangelical Christians avow their faith in Jesus, a failed inmate of early-Palestinian death row, by maintaining a manic grin even while being carted off to prison for fraud or paedophilia. With its impious denial of limit, its bull-headed buoyancy and crazed idealism, this infinite will represents the kind of hubris which would have made the ancient Greeks shiver and glance fearfully at the sky. It is, indeed, at the skies that some of the will's champions glance fearfully these days, searching for signs of nemesis.

Those who support the American *imperium* do not have to respond to such comments. They can simply dismiss them as 'anti-American'. This is a marvellously convenient tactic. All criticisms of the United States spring from a pathological aversion to *Sesame Street* and baconburgers. They are expressions of smouldering envy on the part of less fortunate civilizations, not reasoned criticisms. There is, it would seem, no reason why this tactic should not be extended. All criticisms of North Korea's odious repression of human rights are merely diseased symptoms of anti-Koreanism. Those who rail against the execution-happy autocracy in China are simply being odiously Eurocentric.

'It is a fundamentally insane notion,' observes a character in W. G. Sebald's novel *Vertigo*, 'that one is able to influence the course of events by a turn of the helm, by will-power alone, whereas in fact all is determined by the most complex interdependencies.' The cult of the will disowns the truth of our dependency, which springs from our fleshly existence. To have a body is to live dependently. Human bodies are not self-sufficient: there is a gaping hole in their make-up known as desire, which makes them eccentric to themselves. It is this desire which makes us non-animal: wayward, errant, unfulfilled. If we lived like wild beasts, our existence would be far less askew. Desire infiltrates our animal instincts and twists them out of true. Yet it is because of desire, among other things, that we are historical creatures, able to transform ourselves within the limits of our species-being. We are able to become self-determining, but only on the basis of a deeper dependency. This dependency is the condition of our freedom, not the infringement of it. Only those who feel supported can be secure enough to be free. Our identity and well-being are always in the keeping of the Other.

'To be self-willed,' writes St Augustine in his *Confessions*, is 'to be in one self in the sense of to please oneself, [which] is not to be wholly nothing but to be approaching nothingness.' To exist independently is to be a kind of cypher. The self-willed have the emptiness of a tautology. They make the mistake of imagining that to act according to laws outside the self is to be something less than the author of one's own being. Whereas the truth is that we could not act purposively at all except according to rules and conventions which no one individual invented. Such rules are not a restraint upon individual freedom, as the Romantic imagines: they are one of the conditions of it. I could not act according to rules which were in principle intelligible only to me. I would have no more idea of what I was doing than anybody else would.

The will, however, confronts one enormous obstacle: itself. It can bend the world into any shape it pleases, but to do so it needs to be austere, unyielding, and thus exempt from its own fondness for plasticity. This austerity also means that it cannot really enjoy the world it has manufactured. For freedom from limit to flourish, then, the will which thrusts us beyond those limits has to go. What is needed is a perpetually malleable world, but one without the intransigent will. If the world itself is to have all the free-floating nature of subjectivity, the robust human subject has to disappear. And this is the culture of postmodernism. With postmodernism, the will turns back upon itself and colonizes the strenuously willing subject itself. It gives birth to a human being every bit as protean and diffuse as the society around it.

The creature who emerges from postmodern thought is centreless, hedonistic, self-inventing, ceaselessly adaptive. He thus fares splendidly in the disco or supermarket, though not quite so well in the school, courtroom or chapel. He sounds more like a Los Angeles media executive than an Indonesian fisherman. Postmodernists oppose universality, and well they might: nothing is more parochial than the kind of human being they admire. It is as though we must now sacrifice our identity to our free-dom, which leaves open the question of who is left to exercise that freedom. We become like a chief executive so dizzied and punch-drunk with incessant travel that he can no longer recall his name. The human subject finally breaks free of the restriction which is itself. If all that is solid must be dissolved into air, there can be no exceptions made for human beings.

This includes the idea of there being firm foundations to social life. 'Nothing we do,' writes Ludwig Wittgenstein, 'can be defended absolutely and finally,'[2] a statement which may be taken as a keynote of much modern thought. In a brutally fundamentalist era, this sense of the provisional nature of all our ideas – one central to post-structuralism and postmodernism – is deeply salutary. Whatever the blindspots and prejudices of

2. Ludwig Wittgenstein, *Culture and Value*, Oxford, 1966, p. 16.

these theories, they pale in comparison with the lethal self-righteousness of the fundamentalist. And they can of course be valuable antidotes to it. The problem is that the bracing scepticism of some postmodern thought is hard to distinguish from its aversion to engaging with fundamentalism at the kind of 'deep' moral or metaphysical level where it needs to be confronted. Indeed, this might serve as a summary of the dilemma in which cultural theory is now caught. Postmodernism has an allergy to depth, as indeed did the later Wittgenstein. It believes that part of what is wrong with fundamentalism is its pitching of the arguments at a universal, first-principled, a-historical level. In this, postmodernism is mistaken. It is not the level at which fundamentalism pitches its claims which is the problem; it is the nature of the claims themselves.

It is not as though everything we say or do floats in the air unless it can be anchored in some self-evident first principle. If someone asks me why I insist on wearing a paper bag over my head in public, it is sufficient explanation for me to say that I am self-conscious about my appearance. I do not have to go on to add that this is so because when I was a child my parents told me that I looked like a miniature version of Boris Karloff, and that they told me so because they were psychopathic sadists who took a perverse delight in ripping my self-confidence to shreds.

Nor do I have then to explain why my parents came to be as they were. 'I'm self-conscious about my appearance' is not incomplete as an explanation unless I trace it back to first principles, such as 'some people are just psychopaths'. It will do as a baseline for the moment. As Wittgenstein advises us: if you are asked which is the last house in the village, don't reply that there isn't one because someone might always build another. Indeed they could; but that house over there is the last one for now. The village is not incomplete. Explanations have to come to an end somewhere.

This, to be sure, has its dangers. 'If I have exhausted the justifications,' Wittgenstein remarks in his simple-peasant persona, 'I have reached bedrock, and my spade is turned. Then I am inclined to say: "This is simply what I do." '[3] But what if what I do is defraud the elderly of their life savings? Wittgenstein, it is true, is thinking of more fundamental matters than that. He has in mind the very cultural forms which allow us to think what we think and do what we do. Our spade rebounds against hard rock when we try to get a critical fix on the very form of life which constitutes us as human subjects in the first place. But we may still feel that this is too complacent. Quite a lot of what constitutes us as who we are does not go all the way down to habits we cannot even objectify. Wittgenstein is arguably being too anthropological about it.

Is there anything that *does* go all the way down? For much modern theory, the answer is 'culture'. For Nietzscheans, it is power. For some anti-theorists, it is belief. We cannot ask where our beliefs come from, since the answer to that question would itself have to be couched in the language of those beliefs. We have suggested that one possible answer, though one highly unpopular these days, is human nature or species-being. Nature is not a term one can easily nip behind. Once we have informed the Alpha Centaurian anthropologist that making music and feeling sad are just in our natures, there isn't much more we can tell her. If she asks, 'But why?' she simply hasn't grasped the concept of nature.

This is a form of essentialism, at least when it comes to human beings. Radical thinkers nowadays are thus deeply distrustful

3. Ludwig Wittgenstein, *Philosophical Investigations*, Oxford, 1963, p. 85.

of it, since it seems to suggest that some things about human beings do not change. And they are absolutely right. Some things, like the fact of death, temporality, language, sociality, sexuality, suffering, production and the like, do not change, in the sense that they are necessities of the human condition. But we have wondered already why the anti-essentialists should assume along with the fashion designers and TV programme schedulers that the absence of change is always undesirable. There may be the odd tight-lipped puritan around who thinks it desirable that human beings should neither speak nor have sex, but most of us are not of this persuasion. The more astute anti-essentialist, as we have seen, accepts that such things are abiding realities, but claims that nothing of much significance follows from this. What matters is culture – the diverse, conflicting forms which these universal truths actually assume in the course of human history.

This is true in one sense, and eccentric in another. How could anyone imagine that the various cultural forms assumed by, say, death matter more than the reality of death itself? Why should the fact that some people are buried standing up while others are treated to ceremonial rifle fire over their coffins seem more important than the astonishing truth that none of us will be around in a century's time? Which would be likely to strike the immortal Alpha Centaurian anthropologist as more noteworthy? Anyway, the fact that something is natural does not automatically make it acceptable, which is part of what the anti-essentialists seem to fear. Death is natural, and probably some forms of sickness, but many of us would prefer to see the back of them. It would be preferable if black mambas could not travel as frighteningly fast as they can, but short of hanging weights on them it seems that our hands are tied. In any case, the human essence is all about change. It is because we are labouring, social, sexual, linguistic animals that we have history in the first place. If this nature were to alter radically, we might cease to be cultural, historical creatures altogether. The anti-essentialists would then doubtless be in something of a dilemma.

The problem with a foundation is that it always seems possible to slip another one underneath it. As soon as you have defined it, it seems to lose its finality. It may be that the world is resting on an elephant and the elephant on a turtle, but what is the turtle resting on? You can tough this question out and claim, as the anti-foundationalist famously did, that it's turtles all the way down; but all the way down to what? As Pascal points out in his *Pensées*: '. . . anybody can see that those [principles] which are supposed to be ultimate do not stand by themselves, but depend on others, which depend on others again, and thus never allow of any finality.'[4] The tormented protagonist of Dostoevsky's *Notes from Underground* complains that 'any primary cause I have immediately drags another one in tow, and that one is even more primary, and so on *ad infinitum*'. What you would need, to avoid this infinite regress, is a foundation which was self-evident and self-justifying. You would need a self-founding foundation. And it was traditionally the task of philosophy to come up with plausible candidates for this role.

To invent the idea of God is the swiftest solution to this problem. For God is by definition what you cannot dig deeper than. He is, as Spinoza remarks, a 'self-causing Cause', having his ends, grounds and purposes entirely within himself. This, however, was not a solution destined to last. For one thing, God proved too fuzzy, nebulous a foundation. He was not a principle, an entity, a definable being, or even a person in the sense in which Al Gore is arguably one. God and the universe do not add up to

4. Blaise Pascal, *Pensées*, London, 1995, p. 62.

two. For another thing, if God really was the foundation of the world, he had clearly rustled the whole thing up in a moment of criminal negligence and had a lot of hard explaining to do. Quite why he needed to provide us with cholera as well as chloroform was not entirely obvious. The whole project had clearly been insanely over-ambitious and required some radical retooling. It was hard to reconcile the idea of God with small children having their skin burnt off by chemical weapons.

There were reasons other than God's apparent brutality, however, which brought him into disrepute. What you needed from a foundation was a sense of why things were necessarily as they were; but God was no adequate answer to this. Indeed, in one sense he was exactly the opposite. The idea of Creation meant that he had manufactured the world just for the hell of it, as a quick glance around the place is enough to confirm. He did not need to do it. Being God, he does not need to do anything. The creation is wholly contingent. It might just as well not have been. This is one thing that is meant by the claim that God transcends his world. God is the reason why there is anything at all rather than just nothing. But that is just a way of saying that there really isn't any reason.

Besides, God had committed a fatal blunder in fashioning the universe. He had made it so that it could be free, meaning autonomous of himself. For the world to be his creation meant that it shared in his own freedom, and thus was self-determining. And this applied especially to human beings, whose freedom was an image of his own. It was in this sense that they were fashioned in his likeness – an odd claim otherwise, since God presumably does not have ovaries or toe-nails. Paradoxically, it was by being dependent on him that they were free. Freedom, however, cannot be represented. It is elusive, quicksilver stuff which slips through our fingers and refuses to be imaged. To define it is to destroy it.

So the world had its foundation in freedom – but this seemed like having no foundation at all. And if it worked all by itself, then where was the need for a God? We could develop instead a discourse which accepted the world in its autonomy and left aside its absentee manufacturer. This was known as science. God had been made redundant by his own creation. There was simply no point in retaining him on the payroll. It was his rashly big-hearted decision to allow the world to operate all by itself that had finally done for him. Like an inventor whose scheme for an indestructible brand of leather is bought up by a shoe company and consigned to the flames, he had been too clever by half and had done himself out of a job.

There was, however, no shortage of alternative candidates for foundations. Nature, Reason, History, Spirit, Power, Production, Desire: the modern age has seen all of these come, and in most cases go. They were all in their different ways narratives of Man. Man could serve as the new foundation. But this was scarcely satisfactory either. For one thing, it seemed oddly circular to see Man as the foundation of Man. Man seemed a more promising candidate than God for foundational status because he was fleshly and palpable. The invisibility of God had always been a grave drawback to his career prospects as a foundation, leading many to the not unreasonable conclusion that it was not that he was there but hiding; it was simply that he was not there.

For another thing, Man had to be stripped of his flesh and blood to perform this role. He had to be reduced to the abstract human subject – the word 'subject' meaning that which lies underneath, or foundation. To play this august role, he had to shed his carnal reality. Man as historical was too finite to be an effective foundation, whereas Man as universal subject was too intangible. Since he, too, was constituted by freedom, he ran into all the problems which had already scuppered God. To take your stand on freedom seemed like taking it on thin air. If to be free is to be unknowable, then Man became as inscrutable as God, not least to himself. At the very peak of his powers, then, he was self-blinded. Man was an enigma at the centre of the world. He was the baseline of the whole business, but could not be represented within it. Instead, he was a haunting absence at its heart.

It was flattering, naturally, for Man to be raised to this quasi-divine status. It was satisfying to feel that the whole world depended on ourselves, and would disappear if we did. But it was also a potent source of anxiety. It meant that there was nothing independent enough of ourselves with which to conduct a dialogue, and thus assure ourselves of our value and identity. All dialogue became self-dialogue. It was like trying to play hockey with oneself. What conferred supreme value on us was what simultaneously undermined it. We were free to do what we wished, as authors of our own history – but since it was we who invented the rules, this freedom seemed grotesquely gratuitous. We were absolute monarchs whom nobody dared to cross, yet whose existence seemed increasingly pointless the more power we had. What made us special was also what made us solitary. We were stuck with ourselves for all eternity, like being trapped with an intolerable bore at a sherry party.

So in time Man, too, became ripe for overthrowing, a coup proposed most notably by Friedrich Nietzsche. It was he who pointed out that God was dead, meaning that we no longer stood in need of metaphysical foundations. Cowardice and sickly nostalgia were alone what leashed us to them. We no longer believed in absolute values, but could not acknowledge that we did not. It was we ourselves who had murdered God, kicking away our own metaphysical foundations through our aggressively secularizing activity, which was even more reason for concealing the corpse. We were assassins of divinity, but cravenly disavowed our deicide. And this disavowal was the artificial respirator which was keeping a terminally ill God alive. Nietzsche, like his postmodern disciples, was simply asking us to come clean about this. We were like a couple whose marriage has been dead for years but who will simply not admit it. We were caught in a performative contradiction, our protestations absurdly at odds with our behaviour. A banker or politician may claim he believes in absolute values, but you can generally see that he does not simply by observing what he does. You do not need to peer into his soul. The White House believes devoutly in the Almighty, and transparently believes in no such thing.

For Nietzsche, there was no point in replacing God with Man. This was just another crafty ruse to avoid confronting God's demise. Nothing was to be gained by substituting the idolatry of humanism for the idolatry of religion. The two creeds stood or fell together. The death of God must entail the death of Man, who is merely God's avatar on earth. This, ironically, was simply an inversion of what Christianity itself had taught. For Christian faith, the death of a man (Jesus) was the death of the image of God as vengeful patriarch. God is revealed as friend, lover and fellow victim, not as Nobodaddy. In Lacanian jargon, a Master Signifier is replaced by an excremental remainder. It is this image of the patriarchal God which Nietzsche is out to dislodge, unaware that this is to kill God twice over. We must have the courage to live relatively, provisionally, without foundations. Or rather, we must have the candour to confess that this is how we live anyway, allowing our beliefs to catch up with our practices. What we say must be rooted in what we actually do; otherwise it will lack all force.

In this way, Nietzsche anticipates the movement of bourgeois civilization into a post-metaphysical era. Absolute values like

God, Freedom, Nationhood and Family are splendid guarantees of social stability, but can also stand in the way of your profits. If it comes to a showdown between money and metaphysics, the latter will have to go. The system needs to find new ways of legitimating itself, and has come up in its post-Nietzschean phase with a startlingly root-and-branch solution: Don't try to legitimate yourself at all. Or at least, not in any ultimate way. Legitimation is part of the problem, not the solution. It is pointlessly circular in any case, since your apologias for what you do must inevitably be framed in language drawn from the way of life which you are seeking to defend. The Protestant obsession with self-justification is what is making us ill. Who, after all, is there to justify ourselves to?

There is a difference between believing in foundations and being a fundamentalist. You can believe that there are foundations to human culture without being a fundamentalist. Indeed, quite what fundamentalism is is a question worth raising, bearing in mind that it flourishes just as much in Montana as in the Middle East.

In one sense, everyone is a fundamentalist, since we all harbour certain fundamental commitments. These commitments need not be sound or zealous or even especially important; they just need to be fundamental to the way you live. You do not need to be ready to fight to the death for them – though you can always fight to the death for a trivial commitment, not to speak of a false one. To believe that nothing is worth anything is just as basic a commitment as to believe in reincarnation or a world Jewish conspiracy. Some of my beliefs, such as the conviction that I do not want to spend the rest of my days living in Mullingar, are fairly provisional, in the sense that I can imagine changing my mind about them. It might not take all that much to persuade me that in terms of sheer dynamic quality of living, Mullingar beats Vancouver hollow.

But there are other beliefs I hold – the opinion, for example, that Henry Kissinger is not the most admirable man on the planet – which run so deep in my identity that not to hold them would feel like being a different person altogether. It is not that I am dogmatically closed to evidence which might prove Kissinger to be less obnoxious than I take him to be; it is rather that accepting such evidence would demand such a drastic make-over of my identity that it would feel like abandoning it altogether. But if Kissinger really is a shy, soft-hearted old teddy bear who has simply been misunderstood, this, presumably, is what I should be ready to do.

In fact, it is only because we have those more basic kinds of commitments that we can speak of having an identity at all. In the end, there are commitments which we cannot walk away from however hard we might try; and these loyalties, whether commendable or obnoxious, are definitive of who we are. The commitments which run deepest are only in a limited sense ones we can choose, which is where voluntarism goes wrong. You cannot just decide to stop being a Taoist or a Trotskyite, as you can decide to stop parting your hair down the middle. To be who you are is to be oriented towards what you think important or worth doing. All this, to be sure, can change; but if the change goes deep enough, what will emerge will be a new identity which also has such priorities. Anyone who genuinely believed that nothing was more important than anything else, as opposed to running this line because it seems fashionably 'anti-hierarchical', would not be quite what we recognize as a person. And you would only need to observe them in action for five minutes to recognize that they did not actually believe this at all.

Fundamentalism, then, is not a question of having certain basic beliefs. But neither is it a matter of the way you have them. It is not just a question of style. You do not stop holding fundamentalist beliefs because you express them with exquisite tentativeness and self-effacement, humbly confessing every few minutes that you are almost certainly wrong-headed. The left-wing historian A. J. P. Taylor was once frostily asked at an interview for a Fellowship at Magdalen College, Oxford, whether it was true that he held extreme political views, to which he replied that it was, but that he held them moderately.

By contrast, there are those who have quite moderate political views but who hold them extremely – those, for example, who are vociferous about particular political issues such as racism or sexism, but who otherwise hold impeccably middle-of-the-road opinions. Taylor may have been insinuating that he did not really believe what he was supposed to; or he may have meant that though he indeed believed what he believed, he did not hold with hanging others bound and gagged from the rafters while he hectored them about his opinions. In fact, this may have been one of his fundamental beliefs.

The opposite of intellectual authoritarianism is not scepticism, lukewarmness, or the conviction that the truth always lies somewhere in the middle. It is a readiness to accept that you may cling to your basic principles quite as fervently as I do to mine. Indeed, only by acknowledging this am I going to be able to worst those Neanderthal prejudices of yours. Tolerance and partisanship are not incompatible. It is not that the former always murmurs whereas the latter always bawls. The opposite of tolerance is not passionate conviction. It is just that among the passionate convictions of the tolerant is the belief that others have for the most part as much right to their opinions as they have themselves.

It does not follow from this that they hold their own opinions half-heartedly.

'For the most part', since this is not of course to suggest that anyone is at liberty to argue anything they like. Almost nobody believes in free speech. People who publicly accuse other people of being war criminals without a shred of evidence may be justly prosecuted. The difference between fundamentalists and their critics is not one over censorship, since there is hardly anyone who does not support it. Fundamentalism is not just narrow-mindedness; there are plenty of narrow-minded non-fundamentalists. Both fundamentalists and anti-fundamentalists, for example, feel queasy about exposing five-year-olds to porno-graphic movies, while many anti-fundamentalists believe in banning the expression of racist views in public. We seem, then, no closer to answering the question of what fundamentalism actually consists in. It is not a matter of holding basic views, or censorship, or even dogmatism. Nor is it necessarily a question of forcing your opinions on others. Jehovah's Witnesses are fundamentalists, but they do not usually force their way into your home with a gun, as opposed to sliding one discreet foot in the front door.

Jehovah's Witnesses are fundamentalists because they believe that every word of the Bible is literally true; and this, surely, is the only definition of fundamentalism that will really stick. Fundamentalism is a textual affair.[5] It is an attempt to render our discourse valid by backing it with the gold standard of the Word of words, seeing God as the final guarantor of meaning.

---

5. Fundamentalism is not *only* a textual matter: it also involves a strict adherence to traditional doctrines and beliefs, a commitment to what are taken to be the unchanging fundamental beliefs of a religion, and so on. But literalness of interpretation is of its essence.

It means adhering strictly to the script. It is a fear of the unscripted, improvised or indeterminate, as well as a horror of excess and ambiguity. Both Islamic and Christian versions of fundamentalism denounce idolatry, yet both make an idol of a sacred text. Al-Qaida can mean law, word, base or principle.

This sacred text is more important than life itself, a belief which can bear fruit in violence. Both the Bible and the Koran can flatten buildings. The Biblical phrase 'the letter killeth' has been tragically confirmed in the contemporary world. When a fire broke out on 11 March 2002 at Girls' Intermediate School No. 31 in Mecca, the religious police forced some of the fleeing girls back into the school because they were not wearing their robes and head dresses. Fourteen girls died, and dozens of others suffered terrible injuries. Elsewhere in the world, American doctors who terminate pregnancies are gunned down in front of their families by family-loving pro-lifers eager to flatten Iraq or North Korea with nuclear missiles.

Fundamentalists do not see that the phrase 'sacred text' is self-contradictory – that no text can be sacred because every piece of writing is profaned by a plurality of meanings. Writing just means meaning which can be handled by anyone, anywhere. Meaning which has been written down is unhygienic. It is also promiscuous, ready to lend itself to whoever happens along. Like matter, language in the eyes of the fundamentalist is far too fecund, forever spawning and proliferating, incapable of saying one thing at a time. One can only achieve clarity in language, yet language itself is a threat to it. Yet if there is no clarity, if no meaning is free from metaphor and ambiguity, how are we to construct a solid enough basis for our lives in a world too swift and slippery for us to find a foothold?

This is not an anxiety to be scoffed at. There is nothing quaint or red-neck about searching for some *terra firma* in a world in which men and women are asked to reinvent themselves overnight, in which pensions are abruptly wiped out by corporate greed and deceit, or in which whole ways of life are tossed casually on the scrapheap. It is unpleasant to feel that you are treading on thin air. Most people expect a spot of security in their personal lives, so why shouldn't they demand it in social life as well? They are not necessarily fundamentalists for doing so.

Fundamentalism is just a diseased version of this desire. It is a neurotic hunt for solid foundations to our existence, an inability to accept that human life is a matter not of treading on thin air, but of *roughness*. Roughness from a fundamentalist viewpoint can only look like a disastrous lack of clarity and exactitude, rather as someone might feel that not to measure Everest down to the last millimetre is to leave us completely stumped about how high it is. It is not surprising that fundamentalism can see nothing in the body and sexuality except perils to be suppressed, since in one sense all flesh is rough, and in one sense all sex is rough trade.

One instance of Biblical fundamentalism might be enough to underline its absurdity. The New Testament author known as Luke is presumably aware that Jesus was probably born in Galilee, but needs to have him born in the province of Judea because of the prophecy that the Messiah will be of the Judean house of David. In any case, if Jesus is to be Messiah, he cannot reputably be born in bumpkinish Galilee. It would be rather like an archduke being born in Gary, Indiana. So Luke coolly invents a Roman census, for which there is no historical evidence, which instructs everyone in the Roman empire to return to their place of birth in order to be registered. Jesus's father Joseph, who is of the house of David himself, therefore goes with his pregnant wife Mary to Bethlehem, the city of David, and Jesus is conveniently born there. By this implausible narrative device, he acquires for himself the right genealogy.

It would be hard to think up a more ludicrous way of registering the population of the entire Roman empire than to have them all return to their birthplaces. Why not just register them on the spot? The result of such a madcap scheme would have been total chaos. The Roman empire would have been gridlocked from one end to the other. Anyway, if there had been such a massive first-century migration of peoples, we would almost certainly have heard about it from rather more reliable sources than the author of Luke's gospel.

The fundamentalist is adrift on the rough ground of social life, nostalgic for the pure ice of absolute certainty where you can think but not walk. He is really a more pathological version of the conservative – for the conservative, too, suspects that if there are not watertight rules and exact limits then there can only be chaos. And since there can be no rules for applying rules, chaos is always close at hand. Conservatives are fond of what one might call the argument from the floodgates: once you allow one person to be sick out of the car window without imposing a lengthy gaol sentence, then before you know where you are motorists will be throwing up out of their vehicles all the time, and the roads will become impassable. Luminously clear laws, exhaustive definitions and self-evident principles are all that stand between us and the collapse of civilization. The truth is rather the opposite: the paranoid principles of fundamentalism are far more likely to bring civilization crashing to the ground than cynicism or agnosticism. It is deeply ironic that those who fear and detest non-being should be prepared to blow other people's limbs off.

The problem for the conservative or fundamentalist is that as soon as you have said 'law' or 'rule', a certain chaos is not kept at bay but actually evoked. Applying a rule is a creative, open-ended affair, more like figuring out the instructions for building the Taj Mahal out of Lego than obeying a traffic signal. There are no rules in tennis, Wittgenstein reminds us, about how high to throw the ball, or how hard to hit it, but tennis is a rule-governed game for all that. As for law, nothing illustrates its slipperiness more than Portia's legalistic sophistry in *The Merchant of Venice*, an episode we have glanced at already. Portia gets the doomed Antonio off by pointing out to the court that Shylock's bond for securing a pound of his flesh makes no mention of taking any of his blood along with it.

No actual court, however, would admit such a fatuous argument. No piece of writing can spell out all of its conceivable implications. You might just as well claim that Shylock's bond makes no reference to the use of a knife either, or to whether Shylock's hair should be tied back in a rather fetching pony-tail at the moment of incision. Portia's reading of the bond is false because too faithful: it is a fundamentalist reading, sticking pedantically to the letter of the text and thus flagrantly falsifying its meaning. To be exact, interpretation must be creative. It must draw upon tacit understandings of how life and language work, practical know-how which can never be precisely formulated, which is just what Portia refuses to do. If we want to be as clear as possible, a certain roughness is unavoidable.

Fundamentalists want a strong foundation to the world, which in their case is usually a sacred text. We have seen already that a text is the worst possible stuff for this purpose. The idea of an inflexible text is as odd as the idea of an inflexible piece of string. We can contrast fundamentalism in this respect with the heterodox Jewish tradition of interpretation known as Kabbalah, which takes apparently scandalous liberties with sacred texts, reading them against the grain, treating them as cryptograms and conjuring from them the most esoteric meanings. For some

Kabbalists, there is a missing letter in the scriptures, which once restored will make them read quite differently. For others, the spaces between the words of scripture are themselves missing letters, which God will one day teach us how to interpret.

There are no missing letters for the fundamentalist. He wants to support life with death – to prop up the living with a dead letter. Once the letters of the Bible or Koran begin to stir, the foundations begin to shake. Matthew's gospel, in a moment of carelessness, presents Jesus as riding into Jerusalem on both a colt and an ass – in which case the Son of God must have had one leg over each. The letter must be rigidly embalmed, if it is to endow life with the certitude and finality of death. Meaning must be watertight and copper-bottomed. Once acknowledge that the word 'bank' has more than one meaning, and before you know where you are it can mean anything from 'proleptic' to 'staphylococcus'.

There is a paradox here, however. Fundamentalism is a kind of necrophilia, in love with the dead letter of a text. It treats words as though they were things, as weighty and undentable as a brass candlestick. Yet it does this because it wants to freeze certain meanings for all eternity – and meaning itself is not material. The ideal situation for the fundamentalist would thus be to have meanings but not written language – for writing is perishable, corporeal and easily contaminated. It is a lowly vehicle for such hallowed truths. There is a connection between fundamentalism's contempt for the material body of the word, which is precious only because of the imperishable truth it incarnates, and its callous way with human life. It is ready to destroy the whole of creation to preserve the purity of an idea. And this is certainly a form of madness. The desire for purity is a desire for non-being. It is to this subject that we can now turn.

8

Death, Evil and Non-being

Fundamentalists are basically fetishists. For Sigmund Freud, a fetish is whatever you use to plug some ominous gap; and the unnerving vacancy which fundamentalists hasten to fill is simply the fuzzy, rough-textured, open-ended nature of human existence. It is non-being which fundamentalists fear most. And what they plug it with is dogma.

This is a labour of Sisyphus, since non-being is what we are made of. 'We Irishmen,' observed the Irish philosopher George Berkeley, 'are apt to think something and nothing to be near neighbours.' Human consciousness is not a thing in itself, but is definable only in terms of what it looks at or thinks about. In itself, it is entirely empty. David Hume, perhaps the greatest of British philosophers, confessed that when he looked into his mind he could find nothing that was purely himself, as opposed to a perception or sensation of something else. Besides, because we are historical animals we are always in the process of becoming, perpetually out ahead of ourselves. Because our life is a project rather than a series of present moments, we can never achieve the stable identity of a mosquito or a pitchfork.

Exhortations to seize the day, make hay while the sun shines, live like there's no tomorrow, gather rosebuds and eat, drink and be merry are thus bound to have something of a callow ring to them. It is the very fact that we cannot live in the present – that the present for us is always part of an unfinished project – which converts our lives from chronicles to narratives. There is nothing particularly precious in living like a goldfish. We cannot choose to live non-historically: history is quite as much our destiny as death.

It is true that in a society which actually trades in futures, the lilies of the field may well be worth imitating, even though it is hard to know just what it would feel like to live like a lily. If we were able to live on the spot, our existence would no doubt be a good deal less agitated than it is. But to bite the present moment to the core, in the words of the poet Edward Thomas, would be to experience a kind of eternity. As Wittgenstein saw, eternity, if it is anywhere, must be here and now. And eternity is not for us. With humans, there is always more being where that came from. We are a not-yet rather than a now. Our life is one of desire, which hollows our existence to the core. If freedom is of our essence, then we are bound to give the slip to any exhaustive definition of ourselves. And if we are also self-contradictory beasts, suspended between earth and sky, the animal and the angelic, we are even more resistant to being defined or represented.

Human beings are the joker in the pack, the dark stain at the centre of the landscape, the glory, jest and riddle of the world. For Pascal, humanity is a freak, 'a monster that passes all understanding'. We are prodigious, chaotic and paradoxical: 'feeble earthworm, repository of truth ... glory and refuse of the universe!'[1] Man, Pascal concludes, 'transcends Man'. Violating or transgressing our nature is what comes naturally to us. In Hegel's eyes, pure being is utterly indeterminate, and so indistinguishable from nothingness. For Schopenhauer, the self

1. Blaise Pascal, *Pensées*, London, 1995, p. 34.

is a 'bottomless void'. For the anarchist Max Stirner, humanity is a kind of 'creative nothing'. For Martin Heidegger, to live authentically is to embrace our own nothingness, accepting the fact that our existence is contingent, ungrounded and unchosen. For Sigmund Freud, the negativity of the unconscious infiltrates our every word and deed.

Ideology is around to make us feel necessary; philosophy is on hand to remind us that we are not. To see the world aright is to see it in the light of its contingency. And this means seeing it in the shadow of its own potential non-being. 'Whatever is,' writes Theodor Adorno, 'is experienced in relation to its possible non-being. This alone makes it fully a possession . . .'[2] To see something for real is to celebrate the felicitous accident of its existence. The modernist work of art, existing in an epoch without foundations, has somehow to manifest the truth that it might just as well never have existed, simply to be authentic. Treating itself provisionally is the nearest it can come to truth. This is one reason why irony is such a favoured modernist figure.

Human beings, too, have to live ironically. To accept the unfoundedness of our own existence is among other things to live in the shadow of death. Nothing more graphically illustrates how unnecessary we are than our mortality. To accept death would be to live more abundantly. By acknowledging that our lives are provisional, we can slacken our neurotic grip on them and thus come to relish them all the more. Embracing death is in this sense the opposite of taking a morbid fancy to it. Besides, if we really could keep death in mind, we would almost certainly behave a good deal more virtuously than we do. If we lived permanently at the point of death, it would presumably be easier to forgive our enemies, repair our relationships, abandon as not worth the

2. Theodor Adorno, *Minima Moralia*, London, 1974, p. 79.

trouble our latest campaign to buy up Bayswater and evict every last one of its tenants. It is partly the illusion that we will live for ever which prevents us from doing these things. Immortality and immorality are closely allied.

Death is both alien and intimate to us, neither wholly strange nor purely one's own. To this extent, one's relationship to it resembles one's relationship to other people, who are likewise both fellows and strangers. Death may not be exactly a friend, but neither is it entirely an enemy. Like a friend, it can enlighten me about myself, though like an enemy it does so in ways I would on the whole rather not hear. It can remind me of my creatureliness and finitude, of the fragile, ephemeral nature of my existence, of my own neediness and the vulnerability of others. By learning from this, we can turn facts into values. By being woven into our lives in this way, death can become less daunting, less of a baleful force which is simply out to tear us apart. It is indeed out to tear us apart; but in the process it can intimate to us something of how to live. And this is the kind of behaviour appropriate to a friend.

But it is not just that death can give us some friendly advice. It is also that friends can rescue us from death, or at least help to disarm its terrors. The absolute self-abandonment which death demands of us is only tolerable if we have rehearsed for it somewhat in life. The self-giving of friendship is a kind of *petit mort*, an act with the inner structure of dying. This, no doubt, is one meaning of St Paul's dictum that we die every moment. In this sense, death is one of the inner structures of social existence itself. The ancient world believed its social order had to be cemented by sacrifice, and it was perfectly correct. It was just that it tended to see such sacrifice in terms of libations and slaughtered goats rather than as a structure of mutual self-giving. Once social institutions are so ordered that such self-giving is reciprocal and all-round, sacrifice in the odious sense of some people having to relinquish their happiness for the sake of others would be less necessary.

A society which is shy of death is also likely to be rattled by foreigners. Both mark out the limits of our own lives, relativizing them in unpalatable ways. But in one sense all others are foreigners. My identity lies in the keeping of others, and this – because they perceive me through the thick mesh of their own interests and desires – can never be an entirely safe keeping. The self I receive back from others is always rather shopsoiled. It is mauled by their own desires – which is not to say their desire for me. But it remains the case that I can know who I am or what I am feeling only by belonging to a language which is never my personal possession. It is others who are the custodians of my selfhood. 'I borrow myself from others,' as the philosopher Maurice Merleau-Ponty remarks.[3] It is only in the speech I share with them that I can come to mean anything at all.

This meaning is not one I can ever fully possess, since neither can those who fashion it. This is because it is not simply a matter of their opinions of me. If this were so, why not just ask them? It is a matter of the way in which my existence figures within their own lives in ways of which neither I nor they can ever be fully conscious. To trace the rippling effects on others of the most trifling of my actions, or just of my brute presence in the world, I would need to deploy a whole army of researchers. This is not only a modern insight; it is also part of the teaching of the great Buddhist scholar Nagarjuna, for whom the self has no essence because it is bound up with the lives of countless others, the product of their choices and conduct. It cannot be lifted clear of this web of meanings. Besides, our lives take on part of their

3. Maurice Merleau-Ponty, *Signs*, Chicago, 1964, p. 159.

meaning posthumously: the future will always rewrite us, perhaps plucking comedy from what was tragedy at the time, or vice versa. This is another sense in which the meaning of your life is bound to elude you while you are living it. What you are does not end with your death.

Death shows us the ultimate unmasterability of our lives, and therefore something of the bogusness of trying to master the lives of others. If I am intractable to myself, I can hardly demand instant pliability from others. Only by not mistreating oneself – by accepting that you can have no final dominion over yourself, that you are a stranger to yourself – can your dealings with yourself be a model for your dealings with others. One would not wish to be treated by some other people in the way they treat themselves. And this means renouncing the death-dealing ideology of the will.

This is just what the fundamentalist is unable to do. He cannot accept contingency. His life anticipates death, but in all the wrong ways. Far from the reality of death loosening his neurotic grip on life, it tightens it to a white-knuckled intensity. The fundamentalist tries to outwit death by the crafty strategy of projecting its absolutism on to life, thus making life itself eternal and imperishable. But is it then life the fundamentalist is in love with, or death? We have to find a way of living with non-being without being in love with it, since being in love with it is the duplicitous work of the death drive. It is the death drive which cajoles us into tearing ourselves apart in order to achieve the absolute security of nothingness. Non-being is the ultimate purity. It has the unblemishedness of all negation, the perfection of a blank page.

There is, then, a profound paradox to fundamentalism. On the one hand it is terrified of non-being, of the sheer sprawling gratuitousness of the material world, and wants to seal the fissures in this ramshackle structure with a stuffing of first principles, fixed meanings and self-evident truths. The world's contingency, its improvised air, reminds it intolerably of the fact that it could easily not exist. Fundamentalism is fearful of nihilism, having failed to notice that nihilism is simply the mirror-image of its own absolutism. The nihilist is almost always a disenchanted absolutist, the rebellious Oedipal child of the metaphysical father. Like his father, he believes that if values are not absolute, there are no values at all. If father was wrong, then nobody else can be right.

There is, however, a deeper affinity between nihilism and fundamentalism. If fundamentalism detests non-being, it also is allured by the prospect of it, since nothing could be less open to misinterpretation. Non-being is the enemy of instability and ambiguity. You cannot argue over its content, since it has no content at all. It is as absolute and unmistakable as the moral law, as unequivocal as a cypher. The fundamentalist is an ascetic, who wants to purge the world of surplus matter. In doing so, he can cleanse it of its sickening arbitrariness and reduce it to strict necessity. The ascetic is revolted by the monstrous fecundity of matter, and is thus a prey to nothingness. For him, there is simply too much being around the place, not least – from the viewpoint of the Islamic fundamentalist – in the West.

The ascetic can find nothing around him but an obscene excess of matter, gorging upon itself in an orgy of consumerism. (US fundamentalists are somewhat less troubled by this excess of matter, some of which they are rather keen on eating.) Like some ghastly ectoplasm, this obese stuff oozes over the edge of every space and crams itself into every crevice. Its infinity is a grisly parody of immortality, and its dynamism only serves to conceal its deathliness. Death reduces us to sheer meaningless stuff, a condition which the commodity prefigures. For all its flashy eroticism, the commodity is an allegory of death.

If all this proliferating stuff is contingent – if there is no reason for its existence in the first place – then there seems nothing to stop you from blowing a big hole in it. This is the project of the first suicide bomber in English literature, the crazed anarchist professor of Joseph Conrad's novel *The Secret Agent*. It is the obscenity of purposeless matter which the professor is out to destroy. Perhaps the first, catastrophic emergence of matter was itself the Fall. Perhaps the Fall and Creation coincide, so that only the violent obliteration of what exists will redeem us. The professor is an exterminating angel who is in love with annihilation for its own sake. His destruction is thus a mirror-image of the Creation, which is equally an end in itself.

The death drive is not a purposeful narrative, but the ruin of all narrative. It destroys simply for the obscene pleasure of it. The perfect terrorist is a kind of Dadaist, striking not at this or that bit of meaning but at meaning as such. It is non-sense, he believes, which society cannot stomach – events so extravagantly motiveless that they liquidate meaning by beggaring speech. Or they are acts whose meaning could be understood only on the other side of an inconceivable transformation of everything we do – one so absolute that it would be an image of death itself.

It is possible to see this simultaneous love and hatred of non-being in the narrative of Nazism. On the one hand, the Nazis were in love with death and non-being, gripped by a frenzy of destruction and dissolution. They destroyed Jews just for the hell of it, not for any overriding military or political purpose. On the other hand, they murdered them because they seemed to embody a frightful non-being which they feared and detested. They feared it because it signified a dreadful non-being inside themselves. If Nazism was stuffed full of swollen rhetoric and extravagant idealism, it was also nauseously empty.

It thus presented what might be called the two faces of evil. The fact that the word 'evil' has become popular in the White House as a way of shutting down analysis should not deter us from taking it seriously. Liberals tend to underplay evil, whereas conservatives tend to overestimate it. Some postmodernists, on the other hand, know of it mainly from horror movies. The conservatives are surely right to resist the liberal rationalists and sentimental humanists who seek to underrate the reality of evil. They point to its terrifying, obscene, traumatic nature, its implacable malice, its nihilistic mockery, its cynical resistance to being cajoled or persuaded. For their part, the liberals are surely right to claim that there is nothing necessarily transcendent going on here. Nothing could be more mundane than evil, which is not to say more common. Even a mild deprivation of parental love can be enough to turn us into monsters.

There is a kind of evil which is mysterious because its motive seems not to be to destroy specific beings for specific reasons, but to negate being as such. Shakespeare's Iago seems to fall into this rare category. Hannah Arendt speculates that the Holocaust was not so much a question of killing human beings for human reasons, as of seeking to annihilate the concept of the human as such.[4] This sort of evil is a Satanic parody of the divine, finding in the act of destruction the sort of orgasmic release which one can imagine God finding in the act of creation. It is evil as nihilism – a cackle of mocking laughter at the whole solemnly farcical assumption that anything merely human could ever matter. In its vulgarly knowing way, it delights in unmasking human value as a pretentious sham. It is a raging, vindictive fury at existence as

4. See Richard J. Bernstein, *Radical Evil*, Cambridge, 2000, p. 215.

such. It is the evil of the Nazi death camps rather than of a hired assassin, or even of a massacre carried out for some political end. It is not the same kind of evil as most terrorism, which is malign but which has a point.

The other face of evil appears exactly the opposite. This kind of evil wants to destroy non-being rather than create it. It sees non-being as slimy, impure and insidious, a nameless threat to one's integrity of selfhood. This dreadful infiltration of one's identity has no palpable form in itself, and thus provokes paranoia in its supposed victims. It is everywhere and nowhere. It therefore breeds a desire to lend this hideous force a local name and habitation. The names are in fact legion: Jew, Arab, Communist, woman, homosexual, or indeed most permutations of the set. This is evil as seen from the standpoint of those who have a surfeit of being rather than an insufficiency of it. They cannot accept the unspeakable truth that the slimy, contagious stuff they wage war upon, far from being alien, is as close to them as breathing. Non-being is what we are made of. Above all, they cannot acknowledge desire, since to desire is to lack. Instead of holding fast to their desire, they stuff it full of fetishes. To do this is also to disavow the purest vacancy of all, death, which the hollow at the heart of our longing prefigures.

Perhaps this can help to explain why so many were murdered in the Holocaust. There is a diabolical attraction in the idea of absolute destruction. The perverse perfection of the scheme, the unflawed purity of it, the lack of messy loose ends or contingent left-overs, is what seduces the nihilistic mind. In any case, to leave even the slightest fragment of this non-being intact is to allow it to spawn and smother you once more. The trouble is that non-being, by definition, cannot be destroyed. The entire enterprise is insanely self-defeating, as you try to exterminate non-being by creating even more of the stuff around you.

Caught in this savagely despairing circle, the whole project is incapable of coming to an end, which is another reason why it devours so many lives. A further reason is that the urge to annihilate is really in love with itself – rather as the drive to accumulate ends up by taking itself as the object of its own desire, tossing aside the various objects it stumbles across like a sulky child, and reaping satisfaction only from its own perpetual motion. In any case, as long as you are alive, you will never be able to extinguish the non-being at the heart of yourself.

The kind of evil which fears for its own fullness of being involves a megalomaniac overvaluing of the self. Hell is the living death of those who regard themselves as too valuable to die. Whereas the kind of evil which reaps obscene delight from the dissolution of the self, fuelled as it is by what Freud knows as the death drive, seeks to expunge value itself. In the epoch of modernity, these two drives become lethally intertwined – for the point about the rampantly assertive will, the sovereign source of all value, is that it crushes the things around it to nothing, and thus leaves them worthless and depleted. It is this deadly combination of voluntarism and nihilism which among other things characterizes the modern era. There is a stark image of it in Gerald Crich of D. H. Lawrence's novel *Women in Love*, an animated vacancy leashed together only by the sheer inward force of his will-power. The manic affirmation of the self becomes a defence against its sweetly seductive emptiness. Evil is just this dialectic pressed to a horrific extreme.

The typical modern dilemma, in short, is that both expressing and repressing the death drive leave you drained of being. Indeed, the rapacious will is just the death drive turned outwards, a way of cheating death which flees straight into its alluring embrace. The subject of modernity asserts his Promethean will in a void of his own creating, one which reduces the works of the will itself to nothing. In subjugating the world around it, the will abolishes all constraints upon its own action, but in the same act undercuts its own heroic projects. When all is permitted, nothing is valuable. The godlike self is the one most anguished in its solitude. Postmodernism likewise dissolves away constraints, but it breaks the deathly circuit of nihilism and voluntarism by liquefying the will as well. The autonomous self is dismantled, as freedom is detached from the dominative will and relocated in the play of desire.

The two faces of evil are secretly one. What they have in common is a horror of impurity. It is just that this can sometimes present itself as an unspeakable slime which invades your fullness of being, and sometimes as the sickening surplus of being itself. For those who feel that being itself is obscenely spawning, purity lies in non-being. Their desire, to adopt Wittgenstein's words, is to scramble from the rough ground to the pure ice.

The fundamentalist, of course, is not necessarily evil. But he reaches for his watertight principles because he feels an abyss of non-being yawning beneath his feet. It is the unbearable lightness of being which causes him to feel so heavy. The most popular alternative to fundamentalism at the moment is some form of pragmatism. Indeed, the United States is split down the middle between the two. But to pit the latter against the former is in some ways like proposing oxygen as a palliative to fire. Pragmatism may usefully counter the bigotry of fundamentalism, but it also helps to breed it. It is because a pragmatic social order spurns fundamental values, riding roughshod over people's pieties and traditional allegiances, that men and women begin to assert their identities so virulently. Family values and sex for sale are sides of the same coin. For every corporation executive in search of a fresh corner of the globe to exploit, there is a nationalist thug who is prepared to kill to keep him out.

In any case, states which worship the anarchy of the market-place need to secrete a few absolute values up their sleeve. The more devastation and instability an unbridled market creates, the more illiberal a state you need to contain it. As freedom comes to be defended by more brutally authoritarian means, the gap between what you actually do and what you claim to believe in grows disablingly apparent. This is not a problem for the kind of Islamic fundamentalism which simply wants a brutally benighted state, rather than enlightened values defended by increasingly benighted means.

When the very foundations of your civilization are literally under fire, however, pragmatism in the theoretical sense of the word seems altogether too lightweight, laid-back a response. What is necessary instead is to oppose a bad sense of non-being with a good one. We have seen that there is a fascination with non-being, as well as a disavowal of it, which are typical of certain kinds of evil. But there is another sense of non-being which is constructive rather than corrosive. One recalls the Irish novelist Laurence Sterne putting in a good word for the idea of nothing, considering, as he remarks, 'what worse things there are in the world'. There is a fertile form of dissolution as well as a sinister one. It can be glimpsed in Marx's reference to the proletariat as a 'class which is the dissolution of all classes', signifying as it does 'a total loss of humanity'. It represents the 'non-being' of those who have been shut out of the current system, who have no real stake in it, and who thus serve as an empty signifier of an alternative future. And this is a constantly growing population.

It is, to be sure, exactly among the wretched and dispossessed that fundamentalism finds its most fertile breeding ground. In the figure of the suicide bomber, the non-being of dispossession turns into a more deathly kind of negation. The suicide bomber does not shift from despair to hope; his weapon is despair itself.

There is an ancient tragic faith that strength flows from the very depths of abjection. Those who fall to the bottom of the system are in a sense free of it, and thus at liberty to build an alternative. If you can fall no further you can only move upwards, plucking new life from the jaws of defeat. To have nothing to lose is to be formidably powerful. Yet it is clear that this tragic freedom can take on destructive forms like terrorism quite as much as it can lead to more positive currents of social change.

Our present political order is based upon the non-being of human deprivation. What we need to replace it with is a political order which is also based upon non-being – but non-being as an awareness of human frailty and unfoundedness. Only this can stem the hubris to which fundamentalism is a desperate, diseased reaction. Tragedy reminds us of how hard it is, in confronting non-being, not to undo ourselves in the process. How can one look upon that horror and live? At the same time, it reminds us that a way of life which lacks the courage to make this traumatic encounter finally lacks the strength to survive. Only through encountering this failure can it flourish. The non-being at the heart of us is what disturbs our dreams and flaws our projects. But it is also the price we pay for the chance of a brighter future. It is the way we keep faith with the open-ended nature of humanity, and is thus a source of hope.

We can never be 'after theory', in the sense that there can be no reflective human life without it. We can simply run out of particular styles of thinking, as our situation changes. With the launch of a new global narrative of capitalism, along with the so-called war on terror, it may well be that the style of thinking known as postmodernism is now approaching an end. It was, after all, the theory which assured us that grand narratives were a thing of the past. Perhaps we will be able to see it, in retrospect, as one of the little narratives of which it has been so fond. This, however, presents cultural theory with a fresh challenge. If it is to engage with an ambitious global history, it must have answerable resources of its own, equal in depth and scope to the situation it confronts. It cannot afford simply to keep recounting the same narratives of class, race and gender, indispensable as these topics are. It needs to chance its arm, break out of a rather stifling orthodoxy and explore new topics, not least those of which it has so far been unreasonably shy. This book has been an opening move in that inquiry.

Postscript

Since September 11, a number of anti-theoretical terms have been in vogue in the United States. They include 'evil', 'freedom-loving', 'bad men', 'patriot' and 'anti-American'. These terms are anti-theoretical because they are invitations to shut down thought. Or indeed, in some cases, imperious commands to do so. They are well-thumbed tokens which serve in place of thought, automated reactions which make do for the labour of analysis. Such language is not necessarily mistaken in suggesting that some events are evil, or some men are bad, or that freedom is a capacity to be prized. It is just that the force of these terms is to suggest that there is absolutely no more to be said. Discussion must at all costs remain on the level of the ready tag, the moralistic outcry, the pious rejoinder, the shopworn phrase. Theory – which means, in this context, the taxing business of trying to grasp what is actually going on – is unpatriotic. It is the prerogative of soft-spoken, long-haired intellectuals, most of whom are no doubt in cahoots with al-Qa'ida.

This is a pity, since unless the United States is able to do some hard thinking about the world, it is not at all certain that the world will be around for that much longer. This would certainly save us all the unpleasant necessity of hard thought, since there would then be nothing to think about; but there are probably less drastic ways of making thinking less rebarbative. It is true, of course, that some Americans have never quite grasped this esoteric concept of 'the world', believing as they do that it is situated somewhere just south-east of Texas. There are those Americans who have no idea of how others see them; those who have no idea but do not care anyway; and those who have yet to hear that there are other people out there in the first place. For some of them, to be sure, the world is indeed solidly out there: it is what you see through a video-camera or as a flicker on a radar of a bomber plane. For most of the USA's current leaders, as for Dr. Johnson kicking the stone, there can also be absolutely no doubt that the world exists. It is a place where international agreements are to be violated, treaties wrecked, other people's land poisoned, and military bases to be positioned. Those who are understandably reluctant to accept such bases, thus becoming military targets in the defence of other people's interests, can forget about the aid that was promised to them for that vital irrigation system.

For yet others, in the White House and State Department, the world consists among things of an obscure, downtrodden species known as 'allies', which means those who are to be arm-wrestled on board when you need them to help you kill people and pay for rebuilding their shattered cities, and ditched when you don't. It is also that assortment of foreign nations who are to be bullied, bribed and blackmailed into abandoning their own supremely trivial interests and falling docilely into line behind the self-appointed Messianic saviour of the globe. A Messianic saviour, oddly enough, which regards the giving of aid to the destitute and desperate as a sordid, embarrassing burden rather than a cause for national pride, and which in any case drains far more from the impoverished world by its grossly unfair economic practices than it would ever dream of bestowing upon it.

Yet it is an elementary rule of warfare that you must understand your enemy if you are to defeat him; so one would have thought that sheer naked self-interest, to which the current

United States government is scarcely a stranger, might have inspired it and its supporters to work out, as the saying goes, 'Why they hate us so much'. It is, to be sure, a signal advance in intellectual enlightenment for some Americans that this question has even occurred to them. It is a pity that it took an appalling tragedy for them to wake up to the fact that not everyone enjoys being hectored about democracy by a nation with a fraudulently elected president, as well as with an electoral system which means that you need to have the financial resources to buy up Niger, Chad, the Cameroons and the Central African Republic if you are to become a democratic representative of the popular will. (Perhaps some enterprising US businessman will get round to this in the fullness of time).

Not everyone, either, relishes being lectured about freedom by an American political establishment for which such freedom means lending military and material support to a whole range of squalid right-wing dictatorships throughout the world, while maiming and destroying the citizens of other regimes which dare to threaten its own geopolitical dominance, and thus its profits. One is not over-impressed by governments which prate of human rights and announce that the prisoners whom they are busy torturing in their Cuban concentration camp are 'bad' even before they have been put on trial. The desire to rule the world used to be considered the paranoid fantasy of sad, emotionally retarded men with inadequate love lives and dandruff on the shoulders of their jackets. Nowadays, it is the declared aim of a nation which regards itself as God's gift to anti-imperialism.

Meanwhile, the craven overseas lackeys of United States power, most prominent among whose ranks is an off-shore US aircraft carrier once known as the United Kingdom, are rather more coy and hypocritical about the whole affair. Americans have always been renowned for their candour, which means nowadays that the gang of predatory, semi-illiterate philistines who rule them is growing more and more insolently explicit about the fact that it doesn't give a damn for much in the cosmos beyond Texan oilmen. The British are characteristically more two-faced and soft-soaping about the whole matter. Whereas the Americans blunder with all guns blazing, only to discover as usual that they have made the situation grotesquely worse than it was before, the British exercise their dominion in soft caps rather than hard hats, taking pains to learn the names of those they may later find themselves knocking around the head with a rifle butt.

It can be said in Europe's favour that it retains some vestiges of a free broadcasting system, at least at the time of writing, which is increasingly in doubt in the Land of the Free. US politicians can rest assured that the censorship of capital will ensure that they will not be asked by TV interviewers why they have been lying through their teeth, as they might still be in Europe, but whether they agree that prayer is a powerful source of spiritual consolation. The United States has an exalted image of itself, and would be a far more morally decent place if it did not. A touch of scepticism and self-debunkery would work wonders for its spiritual health. The very impulse which drives it to stand tall and feel good about itself is the one which is in danger of tearing it apart. Not to speak of the tearing apart of others, who never felt particularly good about themselves in the first place. It is its demented refusal to limit and finitude, its crazed, blasphemous belief that you can do anything if you put your mind to it, which lies at the source of its chronic weakness. Nations or individuals which cannot bring themselves to acknowledge the realities of frailty and failure – that this is what we all start from, and where we all return – are feeble indeed. Intoxicated by their own self-image, they can perceive nothing beyond themselves, and will thus find themselves in the most dreadful danger. They will become the enemies of civilisation in the very act of seeking to preserve it. Like the protagonists of tragedy, they are caught up in some inexorable self-undoing, as their very strength comes to prove their most disabling defect.

Few prospects could be more admirable in this respect than that of the millions of Americans who, in the face of this reckless, world-hating hubris, continue steadfastly to speak up for humane values, with the spirit of independence, moral seriousness, sense of dedication and devotion to human liberty for which they are renowned among the nations. If it is unAmerican to reject greed, power and ruthless self-interest for the pitiable frauds that they are, then millions of Americans must today be proud to call themselves so. It is this authentic America – these political friends and comrades – that I would wish to share the dedication of this book, and whom I wish well in the dark times that doubtless lie ahead.

T.E.
Dublin, 2003

Index